My Reminiscences of the Civil War

with the Stonewall Brigade
and the Immortal 600

by Captain Alfred Mallory Edgar,
27th Virginia Infantry, CSA

© Copyright 2011 by 35th Star Publishing
All Rights Reserved.
Printed in the United States of America

35th Star Publishing
Charleston, West Virginia
wvvw.35thstar.com

No part of this book may be reproduced in any form or in any means, electronic or mechanical, including photocopying, recording, or by any information storage and retrieval system, without permission in writing from the publisher.

ISBN-10: 0–9965764–0–1
ISBN-13: 978–0–9965764–0–6
Library of Congress Control Number: 2011929276

On the cover: Captain Alfred Mallory Edgar, photo courtesy of Allan N. Clower, Ronceverte, West Virginia.

Immortal 600 badge awarded to Captain Alfred Mallory Edgar, courtesy of Allan N. Clower, Ronceverte, West Virginia.

My Reminiscences of the Civil War

*with the Stonewall Brigade
and the Immortal 600*

By

By Captain Alfred Mallory Edgar,
27th Virginia Infantry, CSA

Top left: War-time photo of Captain Alfred Mallory Edgar. Top right: Lydia McNeel Edgar (wife of Alfred Mallory Edgar), date unknown. Bottom: Alfred Mallory Edgar, later in life sitting on the front porch of his home in Hillsboro, West Virginia, date unknown. Photos courtesy of Allan N. Clower, Ronceverte, West Virginia.

Contents

Preface ix

Acknowledgements xi

One: Leaving Home 1

Two: In Lewisburg 5

Three: In Staunton 9

Four: At Harper's Ferry 13

Five: Leaving Harper's Ferry 17

Six: Marching to Manassas 21

Seven: First Battle of Manassas 25

Eight: After Manassas 31

Nine: Romney Expedition 37

Ten: First Furlough 41

Eleven: Back at Camp Harmon 47

Twelve: Battle of Kernstown 51

Thirteen: Shenandoah Campaign 55

Fourteen: Wounded at Port Republic 63

Fifteen: The Private Soldier 67

Sixteen: Seven Days Battles 71

Seventeen: Battle of Cedar Mountain 77

Eighteen: Second Battle of Manassas 83

Nineteen: "Maryland, My Maryland" 89

Twenty: Battle of Sharpsburg 93

Twenty-one: In Virginia Again 97

Twenty-two: Fredericksburg 103

Twenty-three: Second Furlough..109

Twenty-four: A Digression: The Battle of Lewisburg...............113

Twenty-five: Battle of Chancellorsville and
Jackson's Death..119

Twenty-six: Gettysburg 127

Twenty-seven: Captured at Spotsylvania Court House 135

Twenty-eight: Prison Life..141

Twenty-nine: Returning Home 151

Appendix A: Letter from Illinois Relative While
Prisoner of War..155

Appendix B: Post-War Love Letter to Lydia McNeel 157

Appendix C: Obituary of Captain Alfred Mallory Edgar 161

Appendix D: Alfred Mallory Edgar, Service Record................165

Appendix E: Service of the 27th Virginia Infantry, CSA 167

Appendix F: The Edgar House Today:
The Edgarton Inn Bed and Breakfast 169

Preface

Alfred Mallory Edgar was born on July 10, 1837, in Greenbrier County, West Virginia, the son of Archer Edgar and Nancy Howe Pearis. Their mill, known as Edgar's Mill, is now the site of present day Ronceverte, West Virginia. At the outbreak of the Civil War, the family owned ten slaves, five males and five females, ranging in age from 7 to 39 years old.

On May 9, 1861, at 23 years of age, Alfred volunteered for service in the Greenbrier Rifles, which would become part of the 27th Virginia Infantry, a regiment in the famous Stonewall Brigade of the Confederate Army. The Stonewall Brigade received their name from their legendary commander, General Thomas J. "Stonewall" Jackson. The 27th Virginia fought in many of the major campaigns and battles of the Civil War, including First Manassas, the 1862 Shenandoah Valley Campaign, Antietam, Fredericksburg, Chancellorsville, Gettysburg, and the 1864 battles of the Wilderness. Edgar was wounded in the left shoulder at the Bloody Angle at Spotsylvania Court House, Virginia, on May 12, 1864, and was made a prisoner of war. He was sent to Fort Delaware until he became part of a group that would be known as The Immortal 600. This group of Confederate officers were taken to Morris Island, South Carolina, at the entrance to Charleston Harbor, and exposed to enemy artillery fire for 45 days in an attempt to silence the Confederate gunners manning Fort Sumter. This was in retaliation for the Confederate Army imprisoning 50 Union Army officers and using them as human shields against federal artillery in the city of Charleston, in an attempt to stop Union artillery from firing upon the city. Edgar was finally released on June 16, 1865.

In June, 1875, he married Lydia McNeel, daughter of Col. Paul McNeel, whom he had met while a student at the old Lewisburg Academy. They settled at Hillsboro in Pocahontas County, West Virginia, where he was a farmer and stockman. Captain Edgar died in Pocahontas County on October 8, 1913, and is buried in the McNeel Cemetery.

Later in life, he wrote his reminiscences of the war. This work presents those memoirs with only minimal editing. It is the compelling personal account of a young Confederate soldier describing his dramatic experience in the Civil War and its impact on his life, family, and community.

Special gratitude is extended to Allan N. Clower of Ronceverte, West Virginia, a descendant of Alfred Mallory Edgar, for making these memoirs available for publication. Mr. Clower is also a descendant of 1st Sergeant James Clark Hogbin, who served in the Confederate 62nd Mounted Infantry and the 18th Virginia Cavalry.

Acknowledgements

My efforts to complete Great-grandfather Edgar's reminiscences of The War Between the States are in memory of my grandfather, Allan Penick Edgar; my aunt, Ann Davis Edgar, and my mother, Carolyn Edgar Clower. Each of them worked to complete this over many years but was interrupted by the demands of children, school, work and death.

I have many people to thank for their efforts but I owe many thanks to the following:

- My grandmother, the late Caroline Crouch Edgar, who was the "guardian of the text" for many years and encouraged my interest in the War.
- My brother-in-law, H. Hunter Allen, and my cousin, Moffett McNeel, the only surviving grandchild of Great-grandfather's, for their encouragement to finish the task.
- My wife, Vivian Perry Clower, for her editing, time, and photography.
- My friend and colleague, Connie Pyne, for her many hours of typing and editing which made the completion of the work possible.
- And finally, my thankfulness to Steve Cunningham for his interest; his many hours of research, editing, and his making a dream come true by his publishing this remarkable work of Great-grandfather Edgar.

Allan N. Clower
Ronceverte, West Virginia
July, 2011

chapter one

LEAVING HOME

It is the 14th day of May, 1861. The morning is bright and the air balmy. The singing birds, as they fly through the shade trees, and a few early spring blossoms starting up, over the large green yard at the "Old Edgar Homestead," seem to vie with each other, to make the surroundings of the neat, white cottage, with its long porches, and tall columns, cheerful and everybody happy. But there is an unusual quiet and sadness about the place this morning. The ordinary routine of farm work is, in a measure, suspended. The colored boys are sauntering about the premises doing odd jobs. Among others, Caesar the carriage driver, is fixing up the harness and feeding the horses, preparing to drive to Lewisburg, (which town is 4 ½ miles distant) immediately after an early dinner. But just now the objective point on the farm, to my father, my brother Tom, and myself, is the old flour mill, where we were absorbed in earnest and melancholy interest, as we carefully examine every part of it. I point out to them all the specialties, concerning the various bins, boxes, sacks, and barrels of grain and flour, the building contains. I have been in charge of it during the past two years, and am now turning it over to my brother Tom, for an indefinite length of time.

The war between the states threatens to burst upon our country, and I have volunteered my services in the Confederate Army, and am to leave Lewisburg today at three o'clock p.m. on the east-bound stage, to join "The Greenbrier Rifles" at Jackson's River depot, this said company having left Lewisburg yesterday. Now as we have finished this work of examination and explanation, we walk silently out of the mill door. It is probably the last home work we will all three be interested in for a long time, maybe forever. Tom has led "Old Mike," Pa's riding horse, to the mill "upping block," for him to get on. He seldom walks from place to place on the farm now. He is sixty-two and not in robust health.

I cast an involuntary look back, as we turn to leave the mill. I have never been from home longer than a few months at a time, and that at school. Although I am twenty-three years old, I feel like an inexperienced little boy, venturing out from an affectionate home circle. The untried life of a soldier presents itself to my mind in such a way as to fill my heart with melancholy forebodings that none, but those who have passed through the same experience, can appreciate.

We arrive at the house. It is nearly twelve o'clock. My father dismounts, and "Old Mike" is sent to the stables, instead of being turned into the yard to walk leisurely about with his bridle untied around his neck, to nip the tender grass until he is called for again. He will not be needed this afternoon. My father is going to ride to Lewisburg with me in the carriage, to see me off. As we enter the old sitting room, I find that my sisters, three in number, have my valise packed, and my blanket all ready for me to start. I fail to realize just now, how soon the valise will be reduced to a small haversack!

Dinner is announced. My mother, who is an invalid from rheumatism, is wheeled into the dining room in her chair, so that all the family may take their last meal together before I leave. Everything has been done to make the viands as tempting as possible. But one factor, to make a dinner enjoyable, is absent, and that is an appetite! We all permit our plates to be helped, as the two colored girls waited on us with special care, and I might almost say, tenderness, because they can appreciate how uncertain it is when "Mars Alfred" will sit at that table again, seemingly unconscious of the fact that their race was the innocent cause of the war. We all tried to talk, and appear to enjoy our dinner, but it was only a poor, "make believe" affair. As we adjourned to the sitting room, each one glanced at the old clock on the mantle piece. The hands point to the one o'clock. Time to start! My father is the only one brave enough to say, "Tell Caesar to bring the carriage around."

The "good-byes" must be hurriedly said. There is no time to lose. I must be in Lewisburg an hour before the stage leaves, since I have a few things to attend to, among others, to leave my "citizen's clothes," and don my suit of Confederate gray. As the carriage rolls over the hard, white road, and turns at the front gate, it has a hollow, hearse-like sound to it, as we open the front gate, and prepare to step into it. My father and myself take the back seat. Caesar in front, proudly holds the reins, as my father compliments him on the appearance of his horses, the way they have been groomed, and nimbleness with which they move, cautioning him not to drive too fast, reminding him that time will be gained by giving them their time going up the hill. Caesar answers, "Don't be uneasy, Master. We will be in Lewisburg by two o'clock." The back curtain of the carriage is rolled up, and I look back at my dear, old home as long as it is visible, watching the members of the family, as they slowly, one by one, turn to enter the house, servants and all. Their experience in the next four years will be checkered and sad, as well as my own.

chapter two

IN LEWISBURG

There is little conversation indulged in during our ride to Lewisburg. My father is a brave, patriotic man, but equally as affectionate with his family. And the heart trial to him to see me go in the army is equally as great, if not more so, than it is for me to leave. For I had my share of the feeling that all other young men have, who have never gone through a war, or even lived when and where there was one going on, that going to war meant coming home again covered with laurels and approbation. But he remembered the war of 1812, the Mexican War of 1842-6, and had been personally acquainted with many of the soldiers of the Revolution. Yet he would not have had me fail to respond in defense of my country any more than I would have been willing to remain at home, when the time seems to have come when I must fight for or against my home and Southern Rights.

As we step out of the carriage on Main Street in Lewisburg, I'm congratulated by my many friends on being a brave and patriotic boy, to volunteer as a private to fight my country's battles. I spend a few minutes shaking hands and talking to friends and relatives, and then disappear off the street. In a short time I come out of Mr. Johnston E. Bell's store with my "Confederate Gray" suit on. There are the other boys, dressed in their "Gray" suits ready to start, as well as myself. We hear exclamations of "Hurrah for the Grays," and the Confederate flags are waving. The stage is now standing in front of the hotel. There is much enthusiasm, not to say excitement, on the street. My eyes follow my dear, old Father. Many of his friends are gathered around him offering their congratulations, as well as their sympathy. Only ten minutes now until the stage leaves. I have many acquaintances here, as well as relatives. "Good-bye" will soon begin again. I must go and tell Caesar good-bye, while I have time. He is minding his horses. I grasp his yellowish-brown hand. "Good-bye, Caesar." "Good-bye, Master Alfred, take good care of yourself. I hope you won't have to stay out long."

"I hope not, Caesar, hope peace will soon be made, and I can come home. Take as good care of yourself as you can, and also of the rest of our home people. I have great confidence in your fidelity and good judgment."

"Thank you, Mast Alfred, I'll do the best I can."

By this time both of our voices are getting husky. I move down into the crowd. There stands my father near the stage. My heart swells and my throat aches. Goodbyes all around. In a moment I'll grasp his hand.

"Good-bye, Pa."

"Good-bye, Capy." (That is a pet name he gave me when I was a baby.)

The stage is packed full, inside, on the top, and hanging to the boot. The stage driver calls out, "All aboard," and the heavy door slams. We hear cheers of "Hurrah for Jeff Davis," and "Hurrah for the Grays," sounding through the streets of old Lewisburg, as the Confederate flags wave and even shouts of "Farewell forever to the Star-spangled Banner!" are heard. Such wild and reckless enthusiasm! Time must develop what the end will be.

The heavily loaded stage moves rather slowly up the eastern hill, passing the different stores and dwelling houses so familiar to me. Now we are rattling down the river hill and across the bridge, in a few hours reaching the White Sulphur Springs. Here I get my supper, retire to my room, and to bed. I get up in the morning about my usual time of rising, take my breakfast in the dining room, at the table pay my bill, get in the stage and off again. All entirely citizen-like yet.

By twelve o'clock we are at Jackson's River depot. Here I meet my company. "The Greenbrier Rifles," consisting of Captain R.F. Dennis, 1st Lieutenant Reuben Hurley, 2nd Lieutenant S.A.B. Gilmer, and seventy-five private soldiers. There are other companies from adjoining counties here also. We have now but a short time to receive and eat our dinner rations, so they are issued to us by the officers of the company, from stores of cooked provisions sent in wagons from Lewisburg and other places, for our benefit. Still no evidence of a soldier's life. This is only a picnic!

Now the train comes thundering up. A novel sight to some of us. But we are soon "all aboard" and off again!

chapter three

IN STAUNTON

Half-past five o'clock, p.m. We are marched to the barracks and turned in, you might call it. Not much of the military developing yet. However, time to eat comes around, and rations are again issued. This time, baker's bread, raw meat, sugar, and green coffee. Some cooking must now be done, so the utensils are furnished for the purpose, and the soldier's life, in a very modified and limited form, commences. We are all thrown in contact with each other here, and I meet with many of my neighbors and acquaintances. Almost the first man I meet is Colonel James Davis, a close neighbor and friend of my parents, who has volunteered as a private in "The Greenbrier Rifles," and also C.L. Davis, his nephew. W.H. Callison, William and James Frazier, J.W.A. Ford, Edward and Albert Stalnaker, Joseph Gilkison, William Caldwell, Davis and Frank Smith, with many others from Lewisburg and vicinity are volunteers in this company. We are forming a warm attachment for each other, and taking deep interest in each other's welfare, simply because our homes are close together. Yes, home is the magnet! Getting through supper with some degree of comfort, we try to get what pleasure we can out of the situation. Some of us are homesick. The night coming on, our minds wander back to the dear old "hearth-stone," and our dear ones gathered around it, talking and thinking of us, as they look at our vacant seats.

Now the hour has come that civilians call "bed-time," but soldiers must find out who is to stand guard, and which ones can roll up in their blankets and go to sleep. The officers arrange the guards. My watch does not come until four o'clock a.m. So it is not necessary for me to break my home record of retiring at half-past eight.

Quiet soon reigns inside the barracks, and I know nothing until called by the sentinel, who points out my post of duty. It is four o'clock, and two hours is the time appointed for me to walk my beat. After the two hours have passed, I look for my relief, but in vain. I have been forgotten. It's seven before I am thought of. The sun has been pouring down his burning rays on me for two hours, and my head is aching, because of the heat and an empty stomach. I have been accustomed to have my breakfast at six, and that soon after rising. But I'm a soldier now, and must not give up to getting sick, for want of comforts required by citizens. The morning meal passes much as did the evening one. All the difference is, now we have a long, untried day before us, instead of a short, untried night. Another day and night passes in the same way.

I have met with some acquaintances belonging to other companies that are here. One from Greenbrier, beside the "Greenbrier Rifles," which is "The Greenbrier Sharpshooters," and from adjoining counties "The Monroe Guards," "The Alleghany Roughs," and "The Hibernians," which is an Irish company, as its name indicates, and it is a fine looking one. It is getting to be rather monotonous here. We have no drill, but "The Squad Drill," as none of our officers know anything about military tactics. We are not armed with anything, except each of us boys belonging to "The Greenbrier Rifles" have a tremendous bowie-knife. It is not clearly defined in any of our minds what we will do with that, unless it is in Frank Smith's. I think he expects to scalp some Yankees if he is fortunate enough to meet with any. So cooking rations, eating meals, and occasionally waking down the street, is the only variety of pastime we have. True, we have elected the non-commissioned officers for our company, and among others, Charles L. Davis was elected Orderly Sergeant.

Writing home is really more pleasure than anything else. I could lie or sit around on the ground with my fellow soldiers and abuse the "Yankees", or indulge in "fillipies" against the Federal Government, but I never did like to talk except when I had something to say that I believed was necessary to be said. I do like to think, and very naturally my thoughts at this time turn to the prospective civil war and the causes that led to it. When I left home, my father, as well as many other conservative and peace-loving old men and a few young ones, especially those like myself who belonged to "the old time Whig Party," entertained some hope that terms of an "honorable peace" might yet be reached by conservative, intelligent, leading men, who hoped were still to be found in both North and South, and that the country might yet be spared the bloody horrors of civil war. However, the last effort made by Virginia in February through the "Peace Conference" to save the Union utterly failed, and she, so distinguished in history for justice and honor, was compelled to pass the ordinance of secession herself.

But hope will sometimes linger in the heart while the head repudiates it! It is greatly to be feared that the prediction made by a wise, Southern gentleman about the time of the Missouri Compromise might come true, as the struggle for political power between North and South was getting to be so exciting. He said, "A fire had been kindled, which only seas of blood could extinguish. If Northern men persisted, the Union would be dissolved." And a far-seeing man from the North replied, "If dissolution of the Union must take place, let it be so. If civil war must come, I can only say, let it come." Now the situation looks ominously like it had come although it has been forty-two years getting here! But during all that time, our representatives in prominent places in the government were by no means legislating in "brotherly love" and "the bonds of peace," but with bitter and inflammatory controversy concerning certain vexing questions, such as State Rights, Tariff Bills, and others that could not be adjusted to suit both sections, North and South, slavery underlying it all, causing the cloud in the political horizon to rise higher and grow darker year by year, until it has reached the present threatening aspect. Washington saw it rising before the end of his administration, "though not larger than a man's hand." In 1832, as is the case now, South Carolina was the first state to rebel, and was looked upon as extreme in her political views by many of the middle states, and civil war was at that time averted though the mediation of Virginia, notwithstanding that all thinking people in the south could not help seeing that the high tariff levied on all the states by the Federal government was solely for the protection of the manufacturing interests in the North. However, at this junction the situation is far more serious than when South Carolina "nullified," and Virginia had to follow her young and impulsive sister state, in company with very many others out of the Union we all once loved. God only knows what may be the end of the coming struggle. But whatever it may be, I am following what I honestly believe to be my duty. The institution of slavery I believe to be a "national evil," but not necessarily an individual sin, and that the slave holder is now no more responsible for it than the non-slave holder, and if a bloody civil war is God's appointed way to end it, He will overrule and control all secondary causes for His own glory, and the good of His chosen people, both North and South. And that as in all things, He sees the end from the beginning! My religious training has been in the Presbyterian Church, as well as my political teaching in the old line Whig Party.

May 19th. The monotony within the barracks here is at an end! We have received orders to report at Harper's Ferry. It has a war-like sound to us, and has ever since the John Brown raid. So all hope of the companies here being disbanded and sent home because of peace being made is at an end. I have only time to write a few lines home. We go by rail to within twenty-two miles of Harper's Ferry. That distance, we march!

chapter four

AT HARPER'S FERRY

May 20th. We arrived at this place today, and feel like soldiering is beginning sure enough, as it is the first real marching all in a body that we have done. We find about two thousand troops here enrolled in companies only, well drilled and emphatically in a fighting frame of mind!

We Greenbrier and Monroe boys thought we were patriotically enthused enough to fight as bravely and unflinchingly as it was possible for any boys to fight in any cause, but on reaching here we feel tame and subdued compared to these companies. They have been organized and regularly drilled ever since the John Brown raid, and are literally panting to be turned loose on the Yankees. It might be dangerous to even name the words "Peace" and "Union" here, and naturally enough we catch our share of their fighting enthusiasm.

We are now supplied with arms and the organizing of regiments begins. Our company is offered very homely, old "Mountain muskets," which we refuse to accept, an act of insubordination in private soldiers that probably later on would not have been tolerated by military law. But at this juncture our officers were amiable and considerate enough to gratify our ambition by giving us a nicer looking and more modern gun, "the Minnie Rifle." True, they with all other fire arms, had been burned in the arsenal during the John Brown raid, but having been repaired and refinished, are quite as good as new.

Our company goes into the 27th Regiment. It consists of the "Greenbrier Rifles," "The Monroe Guards," "The Alleghany Roughs," "The Greenbrier Sharpshooters," "The Alleghany Rifles," "The Hibernians," "The Shriver Grays" (from Wheeling), and "The Rockbridge Rifles." All of these companies average as many as seventy-five men each, officers included. Now the First Virginia Brigade is formed, consisting of the 2nd Virginia regiment from southwest Virginia, the 5th Virginia regiment from Augusta County, the 27th Virginia regiment from west of the Alleghany mountains, and the 33rd Virginia regiment from the Shenandoah Valley, and the Rockbridge Artillery. The brigade is to be commanded by Col. T.J. Jackson.

We have no variety of occupation now, except regimental drill, dress parade, and eating our meals that are prepared by men detailed from each company for that purpose. I have not cooked any yet. All those who do are exempt from guard duty and all drill except dress parade. This sameness goes on for two weeks, with one little exception, which is worth speaking of, if only to show how very green raw troops can be, and what a severe experimental drill it takes to make veterans! Theory only makes officers and men for dress parade! (Don't understand me to say I think theory unnecessary). But to the subject. One evening, very unexpectedly, there was an excitement in the camp. A report had reached Harper's Ferry that a large, Federal force had crossed the Gauley River, and was marching on Lewisburg, every officer and man being armed with a match box, sword and pistol, burning everything before them, as they rushed on with the black flag raised! This threw us Greenbrier boys into a frenzy! We were going back right then! Frank Smith brandished his bowie knife. He was going to scalp Yankees then for sure! I had lost mine and so had most of the other boys. We went to our little captain, R.F. Dennis, and ordered him to take us back to Lewisburg at once, to fight the vandals off our homes. We wouldn't hear a word, when he tried to say, "Boys, I have no power to take you away from here. We all belong to the 27th Virginia regiment and the 1st Virginia Brigade, and Gen. Johnston is not likely to detail two companies to go back to Greenbrier upon no other information than an unreasonable flying report!"

"But we will go. We will mutiny."

"But listen, boys," said the little captain.

"No, sir! No, sir! No, sir!!!"

And thus we kept on "beating the air," until we were made to understand that we had to either "hear reason," or feel military discipline. This only subdued us. We were not satisfied until another rumor following the first one, viz: "That there was not a Yankee east of the Gauley River."

chapter five

LEAVING HARPER'S FERRY

June 5th. We are ordered to leave Harper's Ferry, and for the first time, the 1st Virginia Brigade marches out in order, with all five regiments numbering about 3700 men, taking its place in front of all the other troops. The whole force, numbering from eight to ten thousand men all told, leave Harper's Ferry at this time, commanded by General Joseph E. Johnston. We started at ten o'clock in the morning and marched until sundown, the first time we have all marched in a body, as a brigade. And tired enough we are, as we build our camp fires and eat our rations consisting of baker's bread, meat, coffee, and sugar. We are only twelve miles from Harper's Ferry, seemingly a short distance for men to march in two-thirds of a day. But as we are raw troops, our officers were considerate, and permitted us to rest frequently during the march.

From this point, we march up the valley to within four miles of Winchester, and go into Camp Harmon and stay there until the middle of July, watching General Patterson, who is commander of the Federal forces at this place. We are commanded to sleep on our arms. Of course, then they are not stacked. It is very evident that neither of the generals wants to fight now. We soldiers know nothing except to do what we are told, but we do a considerable amount of conjecturing as we are ordered from one place to another.

July 16th. We are drawn up in line, offering Patterson battle, who is threatening an early attack. In this position we remain four or five hours, and during the time, the men express their minds quite freely to each other. Some are impatient to fight, as they fear they will not get a chance at the Yankees at all. Others warn them that fight will come soon enough! Maybe too much of it! Quite a few say they will be very well satisfied if it never does come. But our surmises and expressions of preference are cut short by an order to retire from the field. This disappoints the most of us and makes us surly. We think we are running from Patterson. Soldiers are still much like civilians, worrying over things they don't know anything about and could not control if they did. However, we are at once marched hurriedly in the direction of Berryville, and when we get six or eight miles from Patterson's army, we are halted in the road, and the thrilling orders read to us that our little army at Manassas is in immediate danger of utter overthrow, which will expose our homes to ruin and devastation if we make any unnecessary delay in reaching that point. This so alarms and arouses our patriotic enthusiasm that every man of us feels that he will fight until he dies, before the despoiler shall cross the threshold of his home. No one now thinks of fatigue, or of the intense heat. "Victory or Death" is our motto, as we press forward, shouting, cheering, and yelling! It is well that we were marched out of earshot of Patterson, before those orders were read to us, or it would not have taken him long to find out that only Gen. Ashby was there in front of him, trying to make a bold show within his cavalry. When, in reality, he was being left without an infantry force to support him, and in the event he should be attacked by the enemy, could not make successful resistance, which opportunity Patterson would most likely improve, making the situation more perplexing to our commanders.

One o'clock and we are marching through Berryville, in good military order, and stepping to the time of the most soul-stirring, fight-inspiring, martial music! As we pass out of Berryville, we

Leaving Harper's Ferry

look back and see the waving of handkerchiefs and hear the cries and lamentations of the female portion of the population of the little village. For they fear that they are being left a prey to the enemy, and very likely some of the boys imagine they have exchanged hearts with sundry pretty, bright, tearful-eyed girls that we left standing on the porches and in the doors of the houses as we passed through. For ought I know, the girls may reciprocate the imagination. We are now through with this little episode, and are marching along the turnpike. The bands have ceased playing and the military observances suspended. We know that we must march all night, or most of it, only taking time to eat, and are allowed to walk at any gait and in any order that is most comfortable to us. The aim is to reach Manassas as quickly as possible, but our officers know as well as we, that nothing can be gained by marching too fast. So friend falls in with friend, and we talk as we walk.

chapter six

MARCHING TO MANASSAS

I now have opportunity to talk with many of my old friends and acquaintances; among others, my old playmate, John Fry, who belongs to the Shriver Grays of Wheeling, and who is a son of Judge Fry of that city, and grandson of Rev. John McElhenny, D.D. of Lewisburg. In his childhood he spent his summers in Lewisburg with his mother, who is a daughter of Dr. McElhenny. Our conversation was very pleasant as we talked of our boyhood, the present situation, and the prospective future. However, we had walked in silence for a considerable length of time, when he broke it by saying, "Alfred, we are going to have a tremendous battle, and I am going to be killed."

"Why, John," said I, "you don't believe in presentiments, do you? That is little better than superstition! Don't give up to it. You are tired and broken down physically. That is the cause of your feeling as you do. Cheer up, and take a different view of the situation. I have no premonition, whatever, like that concerning myself, and it grieves me to hear you say you have concerning yourself. So let's stop talking about being killed, and put our trust in God, who is just as able to protect us in one place as another, and watches over us with the same merciful care on the battle field as He does by our fire sides."

"I believe that just the same as you do," said John, "But I'll never get through this coming battle alive. I believe, also, that the time appointed for us all to die was made before the foundation of the world, but that time for me is at hand, during this prospective fight. I know at the same time I am a free agent, and could do many desperate things to keep out of the fight, but I don't feel any more like doing it than I do like shooting my brains out!"

Sad, it was to hear him talk so, but he was inexorable. So we talked of other things. It was getting late, and other boys came up and we were separated. But the way he spoke made a very serious impression upon my mind.

We now stop, cook, eat our suppers, and on we march. It is the cool of the evening now. Dark comes on and still we march. Midnight has come, and we are very tired and sleepy, but on we go to the Shenandoah River, which we wade. This, to a citizen would seem a hardship, but to us soldiers it was most beneficial, and exhilarating after so long and dusty a march. We are allowed to remove our shoes, stockings, drawers and pants, the water striking us midway between knee and thigh. We arrive on the opposite bank with our clothing dry and in a comfortable condition for sleeping, which we make no delay in doing. The first orders when we got over being to lie down and sleep two hours! The hour being three o'clock in the morning, someone says something about appointing guards. Col. Jackson answers, "Let all lie down and sleep, they are all too tired to be put on post. I will take that post myself." In a few minutes we are all in a very heavy sleep, that no one but a broken-down man lying on the ground, with his blanket wrapped around him, is capable of. The reveille taps. It is five o'clock: it seems only a few minutes that we have slept.

We get over breakfast, still tired, and reach the Manassas Gap railroad at Piedmont. As we are hurriedly loaded on the train, we are told that a telegram has just passed over the wires, saying that the fighting has commenced at Manassas. This fills us with enthusiasm beyond measure, and we forget that we have ever been tired. Nothing but fight is in our minds. Everything like fear is gone, although we know that many of us, very many, are rushing on to death! We arrive at Manassas Junction before night, on the 19th. We then march three or four miles in the direction of Mitchell's Ford, and encamp for the night. Everything is quiet. The telegram that passed over the wires just as we reached the railroad had no foundation, except that there had been a light skirmish that lasted only a short time. We cook our rations, eat our supper, and get a very restful night's sleep. Rising on the morning of the 20th, Saturday, greatly refreshed, we cook nearly all day, as we have orders to cook two days' rations ahead. The cooks are much elated with their success in the art. They think they can make better bread than their mothers, who, they wonder, never found out that it is better fried than baked. Thus, verifying the old maxim: "Hunger makes good sauce."

So this, the 20th day of July, 1861, is spent in a restful, cheerful and comfortable manner. Yet we know there is a fight coming, but how soon we can't tell. We know cooking rations two days ahead means something out of the regular routine. We sleep some during the day, eat a good deal, and talk and conjecture a good deal. We wonder, as we walk leisurely about, what we will all be doing tomorrow!

chapter seven

First Battle of Manassas

We sleep soundly on the night of the 20th and are aroused at an early hour on the morning of the 21st by the booming of cannon in the direction of Centerville. We have breakfast by five o'clock. The enemy makes a feint at Blackburn's Ford on Bull Run, and we are ordered at once to that point, and to go as quickly as possible. We have made most of the distance when we are stopped by a courier and told that the Federals are crossing at the Stone Bridge, a point about five miles from where we had first been ordered. Then we received orders to occupy an intermediate position. By this time we become anxious for fear we will miss the fight. But very soon we hear firing in the direction of the Stone Bridge, and we get orders to load our guns and fix our bayonets. Now our anxiety for fear we might miss the first is changed to a shivering dread that we may get too much of it to be healthy.

We are rapidly marched in the direction of the firing and reach the battle field at half past eleven. The Federals had forced Bull Run and were occupying Henry Hill, just as we reached the base on this side. We are now formed in line of battle, two columns deep. All the time we have been reaching this point, we have been exposed to a severe artillery fire, and have lost some men, but we are still in line of battle and are ordered to lie down. In this position we remain for two hours, supporting our artillery, and are exposed to a fearful fire of shells. This is now a trying time to our bravery, as well as our faith. But strange to tell, we do get used to the danger, and are capable of being even amused at little comical things that occurred occasionally. One was we had a little Italian belonging to Co. E, by name, Ginnottie, who kept watching all around him to see as much as possible. There was a man by the name of Dych, a citizen of Lewisburg, and an acquaintance of mine, seemingly also possessed of an unbounded curiosity, and kept getting up almost straight to peep. The little Italian, looking towards him, said, "Dykie, what you peepie at?" much to our amusement, not withstanding the frightful surroundings.

As Col. Jackson rides near, between us and the artillery, he is wounded in one of his fingers, but tied his handkerchief around it. He says all is well, and rides on. His horse is now wounded by a minie ball, which missiles are flying about in great number. It was one of those that struck the colonel's finger.

Bee, Bartow, and Evans are all right oblique to us, and are meeting the main attack of the Federal army. In front of us is our own infantry. It is the shells that are doing us damage so far.

Two o'clock. Generals Bee and Bartow are retreating, carrying, leading, and dragging their wounded, trying to get them out of danger in every possible manner. The groans and moans are heartrending. Our loss just now is frightful. The Federals seem to be gaining the day over us. General Bee shouts to his men, "Rally behind the Virginians. There stands Jackson's Brigade like a stone wall!" Just at that instant, he was mortally wounded. Gen. Bartow fell then or probably a few minutes later. Our artillery is hastily withdrawn to our right and now we know we are to go forward. The Federals rush forward with cheers. When about two hundred yards from us, the order comes from Jackson, "Go forward at double quick, and when you get in good view of the enemy, fire a volley, give them the bayonet, and yell like demons." The men obey with the greatest enthusiasm, delivering a staggering volley as they rise to their feet, and then rush up the hill. This movement was executed with so much ferocity that the Federal line recoiled and gave way as we rushed upon them. The fire that greeted us was frightful, but we pressed forward and in a few minutes pierced the Federal center near the Henry House. The men fought bravely and as some fell, the ranks closed up. The men kept to their work amazingly well to be raw recruits. As we accomplished this feat promptly and furiously, the "blue-coats" fell back a short distance, in the direction of Bull Run. Just here an unexpected difficulty confronts us. Amid the smoke and confusion, we cannot distinguish our flag from the "stars and stripes," the "stars and bars" being so much like it. And we are afraid of firing on our own men. (After the 1st battle of Manassas, the Confederate battle flag was adopted, and all the state flags we discarded. The bars were red and white, with eleven stars.) Serious disaster threatens on the left.

We follow them far enough to capture most, if not all, of their artillery on this side of Bull Run, though they have broken the wheels, cut up their harness, and killed their horses. Our zeal had now carried us farther than we had been ordered to go. We discover a large body of the enemy on our left, and are obliged to fall back a short distance to save ourselves. These troops on our left are the "New York Zouaves." They look almost frightful in their full red pants and dark jackets. Some of the boys think they must be fresh recruits, directly from the "lower regions," because no such garb could be gotten up this side of Perdition! We fire volley after volley into them. I find after the fight, that I have fired thirteen shots. We were required to carry forty rounds of cartridges. Just at this time Kirby Smith, who Johnston styles the "Blucher of his Waterloo," comes up with his brigade on our left flank, which is most timely aid and proves an important auxiliary in gaining the great victory.

Now as our brigade breaks the center, and Smith turns their right flank, the panic commences, and the whole Federal force retreats in great disorder. Throwing away their guns, knapsacks, and running at a breakneck speed over each other, end over end, helter-skelter, pell-mell, on and on they go, like frantic creatures! As I stand on Henry Hill, I can see them for a long distance, scattered in every direction, but still running. Not a man stops this side of the Potomac, and some may not stop this side of home. Our artillery fires a few parting shots at them, and the great victory of the Confederacy is won! I afterwards find out that Col. Jackson wanted the Confederate leaders to follow up their victory by entering Washington City, and take possession of the capitol. But he was only a subordinate, and could not have ordered such a move. There can be no possible doubt in the minds of anyone who had just seen what we had that there would not have been any difficulty in taking possession of the city. That panic stricken army never could have rallied to make a successful resistance until a fresh body of troops could have been brought up to take the front. What the consequences might have been from taking such a bold step is not for us, or anyone else, to picture or imagine.

It is now five o'clock in the evening. The battle is over, but to describe the situation or my own feelings is beyond my power. Our bodies, as well as our minds, have been under such a strain so long, that now it is removed we actually feel weak and dazed, and cannot grasp the situation. We have been under fire since half-past eleven this morning. There is much confusion, anxiety, and distress. We do not yet know how many of our comrades have been wounded or killed, and we dread to hear. I know certainly that William H. Callison of our company is dead, for he was close to my side when he fell. I am sure there are many others, and dread is mingled with the great rejoicing over the signal victory. The loss of killed and wounded in this great battle, on both sides, must be very large. Just now we private soldiers cannot give a correct estimate. Of course, the conjectures run very wild, all the way from five to ten thousand. Time is passing, and we are now finding out whom of our friends and acquaintances are killed and wounded, which is more or less distressing to each of us. Joseph Gilkerson of our company, who was color guard, was mortally wounded, and is probably dead by this time. An Irishman by the name of McSheen, and another man named Scott were killed. Seventeen of the company are wounded. Among them are: Frank Smith, J.W.A. Ford, Thomas Henry, Henderson Bell, George Harper, and a man by the name of Johnston. The other names I do not yet know. The Monroe Guards killed are Captain Tiffany, Robert Hamilton, Archibald

Campbell, and a man by the name of Jennings, who was color bearer of the regiment.

With a sad heart I have to say my friend, John Fry, of the Shriver Grays was killed, as he predicted he would be on our march to Manassas. I was almost expecting it after our talk together. I have thought of it so often since with apprehensive anxiety, and shall always regret that I did not ask him if he had any message for his parents, or anyone else. I felt a strange prompting to do so, but concluded it would not be wise as I was trying to rid his mind of his apprehension. Before he quit talking, the thought got to be painfully real to me that it was indeed a premonition of the evil that was to come. It was so different from the feeling I had concerning myself. I believe that I had a decided presentiment that I should not be killed, as he had that he would. How strange that two such extreme cases should meet! And what was it to accomplish? The more I think of his deep concern, the greater is my conviction that there was something on his mind that he wanted to say.

chapter eight

AFTER MANASSAS

It is now near night, and we all try to make ourselves as comfortable as the nature of the case will admit. The first thing we need is something to eat, but upon looking over our effects we find nothing in the way of eatables, only a little green coffee. This we prepare for drinking, and each one of us gets a pint tin cup full, which somewhat refreshes us, and we begin to hope for a little rest. In a few minutes all such hope is dispelled by the appearance of six thousand troops, the remainder of Johnston's Army of the Valley. Owing to lack of railroad transportation, they had failed to get up in time for the fight. They are so disappointed and excited to think they have missed such a privilege, and that we have got such an advantage over them in the way of notoriety. They literally drag us out in the rain that has just commenced to pour down, to ask questions about the fight, and what each one of has done to distinguish himself individually. They are angry, and express themselves in such profane and unreasonable language, that we who have just been through so much danger and have seen enough of courage and bloodshed, lose our patience, and tell them to stop talking like crazy men. For well we know that if they had reached the battle field in time, many of their bodies would still be lying there in the pouring rain, and their souls gone to judgment. We advise them to let that solemn reflection quiet their minds.

Few of us claim to be Christians. I, for one, do not, but I am one of the baptized children of the church, and the serious truth that death, judgment, and eternity are certain is ever before me. Also, that without repentance unto life "through faith in Jesus Christ," it is a fearful looking judgment and fiery indignation. The scenes we have passed through this day are certainly calculated to bring to remembrance all such teachings. Wicked defiance of God's teachings and power is always shocking to me.

It is now past midnight. The rain is still pouring down. Though we do not feel sleepy, we creep under our oilcloths, lie down and do sleep some. We wake at an early hour feeling thoroughly broken down. As we view the situation by daylight, all is gloom and discomfort, the continued rain adding to it. Notwithstanding we have had such a glorious victory, we do not feel very jubilant this morning. The first thing we think about is finding something to eat. We have had nothing since yesterday morning at five o'clock, except that pint of coffee each of us had last night. And to find anything now in the way of rations is a difficult job. Amid the confusion, the wagons containing our provisions had not yet reached us, but we get something we call breakfast.

As soon as we eat, I go over to the battlefield. Horrible sight! I could not describe it if it were possible, but I would like to banish it from my memory forever. Yet there is a strange, morbid curiosity that impels one to look over it and see what can be seen and what we can find. We wander around the spot for a day or two like lost sheep, for we have no drill or military discipline, consequently nothing to do. Men have been detailed to look after and bury the dead, but I am not one of that number. In the meantime, the report that Col. Jackson did sure enough make the proposition for the Confederate Army to follow the Federals into Washington City after the battle is confirmed, but that his superiors in rank disapproved of such a step. I remember just a few minutes before the stampede commenced of seeing Generals Beauregard and Johnston ride up near the front, and I imagine they stayed there long enough for Col. Jackson to make his proposition. At this time, "discretion may have been the better part of valor," but I doubt it. Of one thing I am sure. The soldiers would have been keen for the race. Their courage was whetted by victory. They would have followed like blood hounds, as the Federals scampered off in the direction of the Potomac, if they had been ordered to do so, and would have followed them even into their capitol. It is thought such a thing could yet be accomplished, if acted upon at once. Those fresh troops would be hilarious over the privilege of being put in the advance of such a movement. We boys, who bore the brunt of the battle, would not shrink from joining in, although some of us might start out a little more reflectively than we would have done before the fight. Probably we would be very well satisfied to bring up the rear. But all of this talking and conjecturing about "what might have been," is useless.

We boys of Company E have found something more tangible and joyous to interest us, by the appearance of Mr. Johnston E. Bell, of Lewisburg, who has come to see how we are getting along. He brings each of us a box of provisions, cooked at our own homes. These boxes are most acceptable, not only for their intrinsic value, but also for the association of our dear homes. The contents of the boxes are the first good, nourishing food we have been able to get since the battle. We are all anxious to get to talk to Mr. Bell, for he has a kind, encouraging word for each of us, and can tell us something of our homes. He saw my father and talked with him, just the day before he left Lewisburg. Mr. Bell is willing to carry messages or any little mementos of the battle field, which we may wish to send to our homefolks. Everything of that kind is now considered a treasure by those who had dear friends engaged in the battle. As soon as possible, the wagons containing our provisions and tents come up. (We had left this wagon train in the valley.) As we have been separated from it for several days, we are in dire need of comforts.

It is now the 24th, and we have moved ten miles away from the battlefield, because of the unbearable odor! We go regularly into camp with good tents. We put in our time in an idle, monotonous way. We drill some, but military discipline is very lax and time seems to drag. As we were on parade this evening, the order was read to us that Col. Jackson has been promoted to Brigadier General. We sometimes see him as he rides around, his headquarters being only a half a mile from us. I have been appointed 4th corporal by my captain, R.F. Dennis, and it comes my duty for guard duty this morning. I am detailed as the corporal of a squad of men to guard General Jackson's headquarters for twenty-four hours. During this time I meet with him, and we have a little talk. He is very courteous in his manner, asking me what regiment I belong to, and making a few other remarks, but is evidently not inclined to talk much, and not at all approachable. While he is talking to me, an old farmer comes up, and makes a complaint to him, that some of his soldiers have killed a fat hog of his (the farmer's). Jackson refers the case to one of his subordinates. He then hands me the "New York Times," telling me that I can read the "Northern account" of the great battle. His voice is not a pleasant one, but harsh and shrill, and he does not seem able to moderate his tone. But he certainly does know how to command his men, and hold their confidence and esteem, as a leader and a Christian gentleman. Our cavalry is encamped between us and Washington, and pickets different outposts: "Mason's Hill" and "Munson Hill," points that command Arlington Heights. The infantry have been marched to those two places twice during our stay here.

Now comes the 1st of October, and General Stonewall Jackson has orders to leave us, and take command of the troops in the valley of Virginia. This makes us sorrowful and dissatisfied. Before he leaves, he writes to us a most touching and affectionate address, which is read to us by the adjutants, on dress parade, moving many of us to tears.

From this time on until the last of November, we are regularly drilled and disciplined. We now have orders to leave and join Jackson, who has been made Major General. This gives us much satisfaction. When we arrive in the valley, we find everything quiet. It is on the 4th or 5th of December that we go regularly into camp, four miles from Winchester (Camp Harmon). Here we remain happy and comfortable for a short time in our winter quarters. We are now ordered to a point some five miles distant, to destroy Dam No. 5, on the Chesapeake and Ohio canal. This canal follows the Potomac, and is valuable to the Federals in giving them transportation for their army supplies. There is a large Federal force just on the other side of the Potomac. Although the weather is intensely cold, we succeed, after four or five days, in getting the dam destroyed, but it is with much exposure and suffering to the men who do the work, which is accomplished principally by the Irish of the 27th regiment, who have volunteered their services. Captains Holliday and Robinson go with their companies. The latter is captain of the "Hiberians" of Alleghany County, that fine looking company that I have before referred to. They go bravely into the almost ice cold water, waist deep, and cut the cribs. This job requires a sound body and a strong will. The rest of us, belonging to the Stonewall Brigade, guard them while they work. We are all exposed to a severe fire from the enemy's artillery and "Minnie-balls."

Our artillerists are trying to dislodge the enemy, who greatly annoy us, from a large barn on the opposite side of the river. They having failed to hit the barn, I see Gen. Jackson go to one of the pieces of artillery and fire. His second shot fires the barn and the enemy is dislodged. So much for his military skill.

One man belonging to the guard has just been killed, struck by a "minnie-ball." Poor fellow! I knew him. His name is Bird, of Co. H, from Rockbridge County. After this work is completed, we return to our comfortable winter quarters. Here we remain until the first of January, when we get orders to be ready to move.

chapter nine

ROMNEY EXPEDITION

This morning, the first day of January, 1862, we start on a march in the direction of Romney. The morning is bright and warm, a very comfortable day, much like spring. We start off in good health and spirits, but towards evening there is a great change in the weather. The wind rises, and we notice that it is getting considerably colder. But the roads are in good condition and we make good headway. We are apprehensive that we are starting on a winter campaign, and feel some regret at leaving our comfortable winter quarters, Camp Harmon. Next morning the weather has gotten several degrees colder, and we suffer a good deal. The snow and sleet are falling. The roads that were nice yesterday are getting to be almost impassable for our wagons because of the ice. We have no trouble with the Yankees. When they hear that Jackson is coming, they "skedaddle" across the Potomac. Our cavalry just brush them out of the way, and the infantry has nothing to do but march along. It is extremely cold, and the exposure is making the trip hard on us, but General Jackson shares all of our hardships, and we push bravely on. Our confidence in him as a leader makes us feel sure that he knows what he is about, and that he has some important object in view. We are determined to help him carry out his plans by implicit obedience. The Stonewall Brigade will never go back on "Old Jack." Often our wagons cannot keep up with us, and we have to bivouac with nothing but a blanket, and possibly an oilcloth, just what we can carry. So our suffering from this intense cold is very great.

We are now joined by Gen. Loring's command, and we cheer them lustily, as they fall into ranks in our rear. Loring has charge of his own command, but is subject to Jackson's orders, Loring being only brigadier. Jackson is doing a great deal of maneuvering, which of course we understand nothing about except to obey orders. His object point seems to be Romney. He must be watching the movements of Generals Kelly and Banks. The former is occupying Bath, Hancock, and Romney. The latter has a large force just over the Potomac. Now we are marching rapidly towards Bath and Hancock. The weather is still very cold, and we are often separated from our wagons. Consequently, we have no tents to protect us from the cold. Some of our men have taken sick and have been sent to the hospital. I am told there is great dissatisfaction among the men in General Loring's command because of the hardships and exposure, and that they blame General Jackson for taking men out on a campaign in such severe weather. I have never heard any of the murmuring from the complaintant's lips. I see little of Loring's men. The two commands march separate.

I do not imagine there is anything that could demoralize the Stonewall Brigade in regard to their allegiance to Gen. Jackson, so great is their confidence in him as a competent leader and conscientious, intelligent man.

It is now the 4th of January, and we enter the little town of Bath. We find the enemy has hastily left, leaving behind stores of provisions. But we follow on, and soon overtake them near Hancock, and drive them into that town. The next morning, Gen. Ashby is sent to demand the surrender of the town. The Federal command refusing to comply, Gen. Jackson orders that the infantry be brought up in view, and the artillery cannonade the village. The Federal force is driven out at once. We are now marched about a mile away, and remain two days inactive, when we are again started on the march in the direction of "Ungar's Crossroads." We march leisurely along, General Jackson maneuvering and watching for something, we know not what. The weather continues cold, but has moderated a little. We get our wagons up more frequently, and can be better prepared for sleeping. A good many of the men are sick and are being sent to the hospital. The days go by and we have now reached "Ungar's Crossroads," where we have stopped and gone into camp, that is, we have put up our tents. It is the 10th of January. The sickness among the men continues, and is, I am afraid, increasing. Second Lieut. S.A.B. Gilmer, of our company, was taken quite sick several days ago, and was sent to the hospital today.

chapter ten

First Furlough

We are now informed that there has been an order issued by the War department to furlough twenty percent of the men and non-commissioned officers, allowing twenty days to each man. I spoke to Capt. Dennis more than a month ago to give me a furlough the first opportunity that offered. So my application has been sent in, and I am among the fortunate ones who have gotten furlough.

It is now the 15th, and I will start in a few hours for my dear, old home. The change from the cold and discomfort of the camp to the prospect of getting a rest at my comfortable home for two weeks is as delightful, as it is unexpected. It is now late in the day, and we are twenty miles from Winchester, so it is necessary for us to start at once on our journey in order to catch the stage. Abram Stray, of Lewisburg, and Chas. Brackman, of White Sulphur Springs, are with me. On we go with light hearts, because we are going home. We stop once on the way, and sleep two hours in a straw stack, then up and off again, reaching Winchester barely in time to catch the stage. We take the train at Strausburg, and go on to Jackson's River depot, but we are delayed the part of one night in Staunton. We take the stage for "old Lewisburg." I feel much more joyous than I did as I traveled over the same road eight months ago. Chas. Brackman leaves us at White Sulphur, and we two go on to Lewisburg. Arriving there early in the evening, I find, to my surprise, my father and Caesar with the carriage, little expecting to find me. My father's feebleness is increasing, and he cannot comfortably ride that far on horse back. It is a noticeable coincidence, that when I get out of the stage, I see my dear father standing on the street almost in the very same spot where I last saw him on the 14th of last May. How my heart throbs with joy! He may be expecting a letter from me, but not me. I walk rapidly towards him, and I soon discover that he does not recognize me. I have grown so stout, and my bronzed and bearded face have so changed my appearance, that it is not until I take hold of his hand that he knows me. His joy and gratitude are unbounded. When he can realize that it is really me, and that we have been spared to meet again after I have passed through so much danger, and he and my dear mother through so much anxiety. The first thing he says after our greeting is over is, "How glad your Mother will be to see you, Capy!" And then comes the question, "How long is your furlough?" I tell him twenty days, and three of them are already gone. "The whole time will soon be gone, Capy. Let's call Caesar, and hurry home." But Caesar had heard the glad news and is already coming with the carriage, looking the picture of happiness. He is driving the same team, and has on his same "Sunday clothes," just as much like he did the day I left as possible, except there is a broad grin on his face now and then. He, as well as myself, were almost crying. We shake hands with genuine good comradeship.

"Well, Caesar," I said, "You surely have not been here all this time, waiting for peace to be made so you could take me back home?"

"Ah, no, mars Alfred, I did not stay that green long after you left. We all soon found out there was no peace in the minds of the Yankees. I have been doing lots of other things since you left. I have been up and down this road a good many times, and have seen many Confederate officers and soldiers, but not Yankees yet. But we get awfully scared up sometimes by hearing they are coming."

"It is bad to be scared up by hearing they are coming," I answer, "but it is much worse to be scared up by their balls and shells whizzing around one's head."

Now we are driving along pretty briskly on the old, home road. But instead of the quiet country appearance, with an old neighbor or acquaintance riding along occasionally, we are meeting army wagons every few yards, their guards, dressed in uniform, are all strangers to me. I speak of this difference to my father, who answers, "Yes, it is a considerable change, but we have been wonderfully blessed so far in many respects. We still have protection, though we do not know how long it will last. There are often reports that our army is going to fall back east of the Greenbrier River. However, the wagons we are now meeting are hauling provisions to Wise's Army, which is at Meadow Bluff. There is a pretty strong force there. Squads of it frequently parade in Lewisburg, making a fine show, drilling on the fairgrounds sometimes, much to the delight and admiration of the ladies. Especially is a frisky little company, called the Richmond Blues, popular with the fair sex".

"But there we are almost in sight of home. You will have to get your sisters and Mary to give the most striking and ridiculous incidence of our experience, as regards the report of Yankees coming. Many comical things follow the tragical in war."

We have now passed Mr. Foglesong's, one of our good old neighbors, and have reached the top of the hill, in sight of my dear old home, and I have lost interest in everything else for the time, but reaching it. I know that the family are all well, and it is the happiest moment of my life. I strain my eyes to see if anyone is out in the yard. The weather is bleak, the days short, and it is getting late. We drive rapidly on, and are now at the gate. No one seems to have seen us yet. I jump from the carriage and assist my father to alight. Caesar hastily hitches the horses, and "double quicks" around to the kitchen to make the colored people guess who he has brought home with him. The family has to look at me several moments before they recognize me. The fat, weather beaten soldier now standing before them does not resemble the lean, pale-faced citizen who left them last May. The greetings over, there is much to hear, and much to tell on each side, but a thrill of sadness passes through my heart as I notice how my dear mother has failed since I last saw her. She is more helpless and feeble. These months of anxiety and care are telling on her, as well as on my dear old father. They, nor any of the family, are aware of it. The colored people do not wait for me to go the kitchen to speak to them, but come in quietly and quickly, two or three at a time, to speak to me and welcome me home. This genuine joy is very grateful to me. They all remark how stout "Marster Alfred" has grown. My youngest sister, Delia, asks, "How long can you stay, brother Alfred?" As I answer her, I notice her eyes fill with tears. I remind her not to think of parting yet, but to enjoy our meeting.

As we all gather around the supper table, our hearts are almost too full with joy for us to give proper attention to the viands before us. As soon as supper is over, I move at once that we go and see if my sister and brother-in-law, Lewis Creigh, will be able to identify a fat soldier, with a lean civilian. They live only a few hundred yards away from the parental home. So my two younger sisters, Carrie and Delia, go with me down to "Lizzie's." Tom goes as far as the mill with us. But the good news has already reached them through the darkies, and we meet them starting up home. So, of course, they know me. Mr. Creigh says he does not think I am greatly changed in appearance.

When bedtime comes, I prefer sleeping on the floor in the "sitting room," with some blankets and a pillow, than to sleeping in a bed in a civilized manner. I do not care to be made soft again, and then, too, I know it can only last for a few days. We retire as early as usual, as my father still adheres to his old belief "that it is a species of dissipation" for farmers in good health and standing to be out of bed later than nine o'clock.

The days are now flying only too fast, but still I am very happy. No one ever loved home more devotedly than I do. I am hearing all that has happened since I left, and how the work on the farm and in the mill have been progressing. Our Negroes seem to be perfectly contented. Yet we all know that they are a race easily influenced, should the Federal army get in this part of the country, their loyalty may not stand the test. Tom says that Caesar, indeed, all of our colored people appear so faithful, that he cannot think they could be influenced to leave us. When reports come that our army is falling back and the enemy is following, Caesar is always foremost in planning to get the stock out of the way, especially the horses. Our family would certainly be helpless if the Negroes should leave.

I've had a detailed account of the sensational report of the Yankees coming, as it passed here on its way east. When it reached this neighborhood it was rather scary, but in going from here to Harper's Ferry, it gathered horrors! The first intimation our family had of this wild report, was by Mrs. Caraway, a neighbor. I will tell it as was given to the family by Mary, one of the colored girls, who is gifted with a lively imagination.

"Here comes Miss Sarah Caraway, down the Levisay Road. Her horse is running so fast that his tail stands straight out behind, and her riding skirt is blowing back with the wind, and cracking like a wagon whip. She is waving her hands and crying, "The Yankees are coming, killing everybody and burning their houses!"

The family rushed out to the front gate and succeeded in getting her to stop, promising her to send a messenger to take the news on east. She refused the invitation to come in, and said she must get back to her father's, who is Mr. Jesse J. Levisay, our near neighbor, and from there she must get home if she could, but she was afraid her home would be burned before she could get back. My father tried to reason with her, telling her that the report must be greatly exaggerated, if there was any truth in it at all. Still she seemed much excited and disturbed as she turned her horse's head in the direction of home, though his tail had taken his normal position, and her skirt floated more gracefully in the breeze as she moved off. Many other things, equally as unreasonable as this were constantly occurring, much to the discomfort and unrest of the citizens, frightening weak-nerved women out of the wits, and causing men to leave their work, and spend much valuable time in gathering themselves in squads to do - they did not know what. It always ended in all dispersing to their homes and laughing at themselves and their neighbors for allowing every unreasonable report to cause them such ridiculous excitement. Then for awhile they would become too indifferent to danger, and would be truly unprepared for it. In short, it demoralized the citizens.

Once since I came home, the report that "Yankees are coming," has again startled the neighborhood, and I must needs start out to help fight them, as I have had some experience in this business. So I got an old musket, mounted a horse, and moved forward in the direction of Lewisburg. I had not gone very far, however, when I concluded to hitch up my horse and join the infantry, which consists of a little squad of citizens, mostly farmers, carrying their guns in their hands, nothing definite in their minds concerning their plans. But Yankees were coming, and everybody must bestir themselves, if it was only to leave their work. When we reached Lewisburg, we found it all a false alarm, and we concluded that as Gen. Wise did not need our support just then, we would all go home. I found my horse just where I had left him. I tell them at home how the report has turned out, just as all the foregoing ones had, and we had quite a laugh over it. We all try to forget for the present that only a few more days of my furlough remain, but the sad truth will force itself upon us when I recognize the obligation of spending one or two of those precious days in calling upon some of our near relatives and close friends who came so promptly to rejoice with us over my safe return. I am actually selfish enough to begrudge the time from my dear home, and all the family feel just as I do about it. However, I get through with it all, and my last day at home has come again. I start, leaving the family just as I did before, all of us with swelling hearts and tearful eyes. We trust that a merciful Providence, who has thus far preserved us, will continue his merciful care over us, and permit us to meet again. Caesar and my father take me to Lewisburg once more. The "goodbyes" are all spoken, and I am again in the east-bound stage, on my way back to camp. It is the 2nd day of February, 1862. By the 5th I am safely at camp.

chapter eleven

BACK AT CAMP HARMON

The army had accomplished the Romney campaign, and are once more quietly resting at Camp Harmon. Stonewall Jackson is commander-in-chief of the whole army in the valley.

I find some war news that has caused great excitement in Jackson's division, especially in the Stonewall brigade; viz, that Jackson has offered his resignation to President Davis. I had heard some intimation of it whilst I was at home, but not until I came back to camp did I begin to realize what a calamity was threatening the Confederacy in this offered resignation. We, of the Stonewall Brigade, think that this trouble began with the dissatisfaction in Loring's command, which so influenced the Secretary of War, that he so restrained Jackson by his untimely interferences with his plans in the expedition to Romney, as to cause much of the enterprise to fail what Jackson had intended to accomplish. This thrust seemed to indicate such a lack of confidence in him as a commander, that he was constrained by honor to send in his resignation. But when the high officials of the government saw what was going to be the consequence of such interference with "Old Jack's" business, it caused as much consternation with them as it had with the subordinate officers and men of his command. The government forthwith made concessions to him that were satisfactory, when he as a true patriot, permitted his resignation to be withdrawn, and obeying the promptings of conscience, again took the post of duty. So now all the wrong seems to have been set right, and we are very happy once more in having our brave and faithful commander with us to again lead us on to victory. I believe if he had now left the army, the "Stonewall Brigade" would soon have lost much of its reputation for gallantry and endurance. Some of the men would have gone to the cavalry and various other commands. Some that are broken down in health would have gone home. As for myself, I would have stayed just where I am. There is not a man in the Stonewall Brigade that can possibly admire Gen. Jackson more than I do, but I volunteered my services to the Southern Confederacy because I felt it was my duty, and I am going to fight for the cause as long as I am able, and I can do it just as well here as I could elsewhere. The majority of the men of the brigade think as I do, that it is the example Gen. Jackson sets his men in valor, endurance, and self-sacrifice, that makes good soldiers of us. So we do not complain when we have disagreeable duties to perform. I consider it a most fortunate providence that threw me under such a commander as "Stonewall" Jackson. Inasmuch as I have to be away from home, exposed to all the hardships, and dangers of a soldier's life, it is no little gratification to me that I follow a leader in whom I have entire confidence.

 I regret to say that I have just heard that the 2nd Lieutenant of our company, S.A.B. Gilmer, is dead. I am not surprised to hear it, for he was a very sick man when he went to the hospital.

 It is now about the middle of February, and we are ordered a short distance from Camp Harmon into dense woodland. Here we have orders to build winter quarters. We go to work with much enthusiasm and build comfortable little cabins, thinking we will be permitted to remain here quietly until warm weather. But to our great disappointment, by the time we have been comfortably settled in our little rooms about two weeks (and I must say about the happiest and by far the most comfortable part of my army life), we get orders to cook a day's rations and be ready to march at a moment's notice. While this much surprises and discourages us, yet we hope it is only a little Yankee scare, and that we can soon return to our quarters. But instead of that, it proves to be a large Federal force advancing up the valley, which our small force is inadequate to meet. We watch it for several days. It is the 7th of March, and Banks had advanced within four or five miles of Winchester, and we are drawn up in line of battle. We can hear the firing of our cavalry, who are engaged with their infantry. The enemy comes so near this evening, that Col. Grigsby discerns them with his field glasses, but they do not attack. We think it is Col. Ashby's making such a bold show with his cavalry that deters them.

Morning, Banks still continues to advance in a cautious manner, and threatens our flank and rear. We are now ordered under arms, and remain in that unrestful and anxious position all day, hourly expecting an attack, but it does not come, and late in the evening, we are withdrawn from the town, and it is occupied by the Federals.

March 12th. We continue to retreat up the valley, Ashby protecting our rear with his cavalry, which keeps our army from being thrown into disorder. But this constant pressing of the enemy causes a most harassing strain on the minds of the officers and men, none of us knowing what emergency may occur at any moment. Thus, incessantly fighting with his rear guard, Jackson continued his retreat up the valley. After a while the enemy seems to grow tired of the pursuit, and finally stops and we hear they are falling back to Strasburg, and then Winchester. We are now in camp near New Market. The troops are much wearied with this harassing retreat.

chapter twelve

BATTLE OF KERNSTOWN

March 22nd. We have orders to cook ten day's rations, and to be ready to march by daylight. A large percent of the army is absent on furlough, but at an early hour on the 23rd, the little army of about thirty-four hundred men is ready to march, Jackson taking the lead, in the direction of Winchester. We now ask ourselves why Jackson is taking his army in such a depleted condition to meet such overwhelming forces? But our confidence in him, and devotion to him makes us feel that it is all right, and we march rapidly forward. Owing to the rain yesterday, the macadamized road makes our feet very sore.

Without resting, stopping for nothing, accompanied by only a portion of his force, the rest having broken down by the rapidity of the march, we reach by three or four o'clock, the little village of Kernstown, three or four miles from Winchester. We here find Jackson standing in the road, with his head up, sniffing a battle. The troops are greatly wearied, and any further movement seems almost impossible for the day. But we are told that Ashby has found the enemy in our front, and we rapidly file to the left. We are marched three-quarters of a mile, and are immediately formed into line of battle. The men are greatly enthused. Fulkerson's brigade of two regiments is on our left. Burk's Irish battalion is on the right, and the Stonewall Brigade is pushed forward on a hill in front. The artillery Company E is ordered out as skirmishers, and we are right up on the Bluecoats' line of battle before we know it. After taking deliberate aim, we retire rapidly to our own line. The wonder is that the whole company was not captured, but as far as I know, they all escaped. This opens the battle of Kernstown, it being about four o'clock. The contest continues for about three or four hours with frightful fury, we contending with fearful odds, since we have only twenty-eight hundred engaged, while the Federals have nine thousand. Our Col. Echols is wounded. I fire thirty-six times, always taking deliberate aim. Just here I am going to speak of a little incident that may sound like egotism, but I hope anyone reading this reminiscence will pardon it, for it occurred at a juncture when I greatly needed encouragement.

An officer, Maj. Lacky, belonging to our regiment, taps me on the shoulder, saying as he did so, "That's right, Edgar, give it to them, but don't expose your life too much!" When we first began to fire, we had been dropping to our knees while reloading, so that the upper part of our persons might be protected by the crest of the hill, but in our hurry and excitement, we were now forgetting to take this precaution, and he meant for me to still kneel whilst I reloaded. Our ammunition is becoming greatly expended, but we are holding the field, and the enemy's fire is diminishing, and we see their colors fall. Greatly to our astonishment comes an order from our Brigadier General Garnett, to retire. We cannot see the necessity of such a step, and we feel sure that this order could not have come from Jackson. As we leave the field, we see a large body of cavalry on our left. We know that Ashby is engaged on our right, so this may be the cause of our being withdrawn. As we leave the field, I come up with one of my fellow soldiers, seriously wounded, Nap Holland, a member of Company E, who begs another man and myself to help him out of reach of the enemy, which we try to do as long as we dare. We run great risk of being captured, for we discover a body of Federal cavalry coming to catch us.

It grieves me to leave poor Nat there to be captured by them, but my staying cannot benefit him. The other man has run on ahead, and I must follow suit, being the last man to leave the battlefield. But I take time to load my gun. I come to a long pond in front of me, and I can see some going to the right and some to the left. I hesitate whether I shall go the right or the left. Little time we have to parley, we divide, some going each way. I take my chance to the left, but a good many take to the right, among others is Edward Stalnaker, of Lewisburg, who belongs to Company E. He, and all the others with him, are captured. I just do make my escape. I stayed too long trying to help poor Holland out. I now see a single Federal cavalryman galloping towards me, and I have every reason to believe that he is after me. I hurry along but my speed is greatly retarded by a heavy, new coat, which I have on, and I don't like to part with it. On I run, the Yankee gaining on me every moment, but the overcoat - I'll take a little more risk before I throw it off. I turn to look at my pursuer, and find him within gunshot, so I bring my gun to my face, take aim, and fire. He at once turns his horse's head, and off he skedaddles! I cannot tell whether I hit him or not, but he certainly changed his mind very suddenly about wanting to take a Rebel prisoner! I have now barely breath enough left to enable me to reach a fence beside a woodland. Here I find about fifty men who have been watching the race. "Why didn't you throw off that coat?" asked several voices. "Because I have use for it, and I expect to get much comfort out of it yet," I answer. "But it came near costing you your liberty, Edgar," said another. But it did not and a "miss is as good as a mile." I throw myself down just about as breathless as is possible for a live man. It is now necessary, for the sake of safety, to hurry on to the rest of our command. But these fellow soldiers take the risk of waiting a few minutes for me to regain my breath, and then we marched at a moderate speed until I am somewhat rested. By this time it is dark, but we keep on retreating, six or seven miles, when Jackson orders us to stop for the night. We cook and eat our rations. We have now marched thirty-five miles in all today, and fought a hard battle. Although we have retreated, I for one, do not feel that is was necessary, for I believe we could have held the field if we had not received orders to retire.

March 24th. We continue our march up the valley. Our scouts bring us word that the Federal army is slowly falling back toward Winchester since the fight, and are felling trees in their rear, thus barricading the turnpike. We continue our retreat up the valley until we reach Rude's Hill, where we go into camp and rest. We now hear that the Federals lost as many men at Kernstown as we had engaged. We also hear that General Williams, with fifteen thousand men, has returned to the valley. We now understand Gen. Jackson's reason for fighting the battle at Kernstown. It was a strategic movement to make the Federals recall that large force of theirs from the Rappahannock. So Jackson, with less than three thousand men, has detained twenty-six thousand of the enemy in the valley. Notwithstanding the defeat at Kernstown, the troops have the greatest admiration for Jackson, and our confidence, instead of being impaired, is greatly strengthened. Whenever he rides past on his "old sorrel," his faded gray cap in hand, we cheer him wildly, and familiarly slap his horse with our caps.

chapter thirteen

SHENANDOAH CAMPAIGN

We have now left the beautiful place of encampment that we had at Rude's Hill, and are encamped at Swift Run Gap in the spurs of the Blue Ridge. Why this change, we know not, unless Jackson is afraid of being cut off from the west by Milroy. Our tents are very insufficient to protect us, being only a little piece of canvas put up for each "mess," so small that we can barely crawl under it to sleep. We are very uncomfortable, the weather rainy, and the ground muddy.

It is now about the middle of April. Col. Grigsby is commanding the regiment (27th), Col. John Echols having been wounded in the battle of Kernstown. I have been personally acquainted with Col. Grigsby ever since our command was made up at Harper's Ferry. He was then made major of the 27th regiment. We liked him then, and as he rises in office, our affection increases. He is one of those genial men who always has something cheerful to say when we meet him, and seems to take a deep interest in the comfort of his men. I believe he knows most of the men in the regiment by name, and that is a valuable gift for a field officer to have. It gives him a personal influence over his men. Military discipline forbids undue familiarity, but Col. Grigsby naturally has a big heart, as well as a brave and patriotic one. His frank deportment towards his men does not in the least interfere with his power over them, neither does it lessen their respect for him. He has, however, an unfortunate habit of using profane language upon the least provocation or excitement. I believe he is often not conscious of the language he is using. If he were a little younger or I a little older, I would be tempted to ask him if he knows what he is saying, although he is a Colonel, and I a corporal.

Now comes an important epoch with us who volunteered at the beginning of the war for one year only. It is a severe test of our valor and perseverance that our term of enlistment is almost out. Not quite a month of the time yet remains. I am proud to record that every one of us bravely stand the test, volunteering for three years, or the whole war. And here also comes the election of officers for our company. None of the former ones are reelected. Philip Frazer is elected captain, A.E. Snyder, 1st lieut., and myself, 2nd lieut. Since the conscript law has gone into force, we have two hundred of the new recruits assigned to our regiment, and forty of that number to Company E. I must now say goodbye to Capt. Dennis and Lieut. Hurley, which greatly distresses me, for I am warmly attached to both of them. Capt. Dennis has been exceedingly kind to me. Seeing them leave for Lewisburg makes me awfully homesick.

While here at Swift Run Gap, we get permission to visit Weyer's Cave, and we go in squads of twenty, or such a matter. This famous cavern is a great natural curiosity. This is the first time I have ever visited it, and this is the first recreation I have had since my furlough.

Last of April. For the last week or ten days we have done nothing of importance.

April 29th. We now have orders to march westward; we know not for what purpose at this time. We are having a rough march through the mountains. We now find out that we are needed to succor Gen. Johnston, who has been occupying Alleghany Mountain on the Staunton and Parkersburg Turnpike. As we march along, reports come that a large Federal force under Gen.

Milroy is pressing Gen. Johnston. And now again we hear that the enemy has reached McDowell, a little village on the west side of the Shenandoah mountain.

May 9th. Late in the evening. We are six or seven miles from McDowell, and although the mountain is between us, we can hear firing. We go into camp, when couriers come urging us to press forward. We are ordered to go on as rapidly as possible. We reach the battlefield just before dark, having marched thirty-six miles today. The fight is over, and the enemy is retreating when we get here. We are ordered in line of battle, and advance to the front, while the men who have done the fighting are ordered to the rear. We are too much wearied with our long march to follow the enemy, and remain for two hours looking at the retreating Yankees, as they pass their campfires. The whole scene presents a beautiful sight. Our position is on a high hill, overlooking the town. I may say here for the benefit of the novice, that the attitude of standing and looking at the retreating enemy produces a much more agreeable sensation, than watching them advance. We now bivouac for the night.

Morning. We now start on a forced march to Franklin, the county seat of Pendleton, Milroy having retreated in that direction. Gen. Johnston's command is now assigned to Gen. Jackson, making a large body of troops in all. The Stonewall Brigade takes its place in front, with Gen. Jackson commanding the whole force. As we file down the rough mountain sides into the turnpike, we see long rows of our dead, arranged on either side of the road for burial. This tries our nerves, as we all admit, more than anything we have seen since we have been in the army. I have never been detailed, as yet, to assist in burying the dead.

As we march through Pendleton, we are much annoyed from the burning woods and fences. The Federals, regardless of the consequences to the inhabitants, have fired the forests, hoping by this means, to confuse and impede our progress. The country here, fortunately, is sparsely settled. They have certainly succeeded in giving us great annoyance. We are sometimes almost suffocated by the heat and smoke. They have, literally speaking, tested us with a "fiery trail."

After a rapid march, we reach Franklin. Here we stop. The Federal forces are found to occupy a strong position on the mountain side, so Jackson does not attack, but he has succeeded in keeping Milroy from joining Banks. We are permitted to rest here for two hours, and our inflamed eyes and aching head certainly need it.

And now whilst we are resting, we are drawn up and the chaplain offers prayers. It is a strange and solemn scene there amid these rugged mountains, with the smoke like cloud enveloping everything, and the sound of artillery in front.

Stonewall Jackson, as usual, keeping up his record of playing a "bluff game" with the enemy, wheels us "about face" in the road, leaving most of our cavalry behind to deceive the enemy. Our army is again put in motion. We retrace our steps over the same road. Again crossing the Bull Pasture Mountain, we march in the direction of Harrisonburg. The cry with us now is, "On to the Potomac!" As we continue our march we hear that Banks is falling back to Strasburg. We have now passed Harrisonburg, and are near New Market. Here we are joined by Gen. Ewell's division. It is a fine body of men. It has come from the eastern army to reinforce Jackson, who now has about twenty thousand infantry, besides some cavalry. We now have orders to leave all baggage, even our knapsacks, and we know Jackson is preparing for a race, and then a fight. Instead of going down the main valley, we are marched through the New Market Gap, leaving our cavalry in the main valley to beguile the enemy. We are now moved with great rapidity down Page's Valley. We begin to understand something of this movement - "Jackson is aiming to cut off Banks at about Middletown." We are now near Front Royal, and directly on the enemy's flank. The advance of our army drive the Federals from the town after a fierce little encounter. It is my pleasure to witness this without participating. Our men are entirely worn out with their two days of hard marching. Jackson allows them to rest for the night, giving the stragglers time to get up with the command. Long before day we are aroused in order to march, Jackson taking personal command. At daylight, we reach a hill overlooking the main turnpike to Winchester. The road is black with Gen. Bank's army in full retreat. We now know they have been moving, whilst we have been asleep! The artillery is hurried forward, and opens fire on their retreating column. This throws the rear in great confusion. We capture a good many prisoners, but the fact remains that Banks has eluded us. Their heavily laden wagon trains are in the rear, although they have attempted to fire them. We capture these and save many stores. We dub Banks "Jackson's Commissary." So the only special benefit accomplished by this hard marching is to provision the army for awhile, aside from the prisoners we have taken. We follow them up closely until they reach Winchester. Here they take a stand, and we have an exceedingly sharp fight at close quarters. The artillery of the opposing lines are unusually close together, and each side supported by a strong infantry. After an hour or more of terrific cannonading, we are ordered to charge with the bayonet. This is a bold move. The enemy offers but little resistance, running like sheep, reminding us of Manassas. We have orders to follow them at a double quick, but not to fire until we get through the town, as many of the citizens are on the streets. The ladies of the town are out also with baskets of coffee, all ready for us to snatch on the run. This offering is timely and highly appreciated by us. Something to eat never fails to please a soldier. He is always hungry, and we have had nothing to eat since reveille. This little stoppage, however, has caused us to fall far behind the enemy, and we fail to obey the orders to shoot as soon as we get through the town, for we cannot get within gunshot of them. However, the colors of the 27th regiment are the first to get through the town, and I am among the first boys. The Federals keep on retreating, and we never get close enough to shoot.

12 o'clock. May 25th. We go into camp four miles below Winchester, and stay just long enough to cook and eat our rations; after which we follow on to within a few miles of the Potomac. This takes us several days. The first night we reach this point, there is a report that the Yankees have turned on us, and we are ordered under arms. It is a very dark night, and a terrific thunderstorm is raging. Lightning flashing on our bayonets affords us all the light we need. It soon becomes evident that the report is only a Yankee scare, and we quiet down again for the night. Our brigade under Winder is pressed on toward Charles Town,

and our cavalry attack them before they know we are so near, and drive them out without any trouble. As we are plundering their stores, I come across a nice, new Confederate gray coat, which, needing badly, I appropriate. Had they intended this coat for a spy? Or why should they have it among their stores? At any rate I consider it a fortunate circumstance that threw it my way. Driving the enemy before us, we reach the vicinity of Harper's Ferry. Here we expect orders to attack, and are drawn up in line of battle, but for some reason the order does not come.

Last of May. We now hear it rumored that Jackson's rear is threatened, and we have orders to retire. We find on reaching the valley turnpike that the rest of Jackson's command is several hours ahead of us, retreating up the valley. But we still apprehend no danger.

Later in the day, stray cavalrymen are passing us and tell us that Fremont is threatening Jackson from the west, and Shields from the east, each having a large force, and insist that is very important for us to reach Strasburg before we are cut off.

June 1st. We continue our rapid march up the valley, and are now about ten miles from Strasburg. We meet couriers urging us forward, saying that Ewell is holding the field until we pass Strasburg.

Ewell has a heavy engagement with Gen. Fremont's advance force, and Fremont's line fell back. Jackson halted and sent couriers to tell us to lose no time. We have been marching rapidly, with fixed bayonets for the last three or four miles. We move forward as fast as possible, and are "up" at last, just reaching Strasburg in time to pass before the enemy pours in on both sides. After leaving the town, we halt and rest. Ewell's division passes us in line of battle, and the Stonewall Brigade is left to bring up the rear. If Jackson hadn't so bravely and faithfully waited for us, where would we now be? But he loves his old brigade too well to leave it in the enemy's clutches. This new evidence of his affection for us increases our devotion to him.

Fremont is pressing us hard in the rear, and we hear that Shields is marching his command up the Luray Valley. But our nerve is still good. Ashby makes a gallant defense with his cavalry, and we are ordered to support him, and are even drawn up in line of battle to receive a charge from the enemy's cavalry. We examine our bayonets to see if they are ready. The enemy constantly pressing our rear, and our army impeding our progress makes the retreat very harassing for us who are bringing up the rear. Our army that is retreating in front of us is, in turn, held back by the long line of wagon trains in front of it. Night comes on and we continue our retreat, the enemy shelling our rear. As we cross a small stream, a shell strikes to one side of the road. The regiment in front of us is thrown into disorder. Col. Grigsby stops and orders, "Men of the 27th, stand still!" Every one of us becomes instantly motionless, until order is again restored.

We get only a short rest and again take up our line of retreat. We reach and cross the Shenandoah near New Market before Shields comes up with his army. As we are retreating on towards Harrisonburg, our cavalry burns up the bridge over the south fork of the Shenandoah, so our flank is still safe. We pass Harrisonburg, and on for Port Republic. Jackson leaves Ewell's division at Cross Keys to keep Fremont at bay, whilst he concentrates the main body of his troops at Port Republic to meet Shields. Jackson's object is to fight the enemy in detail.

Sunday morning, June 8, 1862. We now distinctly hear Fremont attacking Ewell at Cross Keys, and while this battle is going on there, we are enjoying a peaceful Sabbath at Port Republic, although we can hear the firing, even of the small arms, to say nothing of the tremendous cannonading. We are suddenly interrupted in our quiet rest, as we are watching a portion of Shield's army that does not appear to be very close, by two or three couriers dashing into camp, and the "long roll" is beat! We at once take our guns out of stack, and fall into ranks with utmost haste. The artillery and infantry are hurriedly ordered over the Shenandoah River, which point the enemy have just taken. Gen. Jackson was actually cut off there by some Federal artillerists, but he, by his usual adroitness, escaped before they knew they had him. He, taking in their situation at once, gave orders, as though he was their commander. This momentarily confused them when he galloped across the bridge to his own division. He knew that the artillerists not having small arms could not shoot at him, even when they discovered their mistake.

We are now doubled quicked to the bridge. Taliaferro's brigade retake the bridge without any difficulty, and capture his pieces of artillery. The Federals hastily retreat from the town, and are followed by our men down the river. Our artillery is ordered lower down on the river to enfilade the enemy as they retreat. We still hear the fighting at Cross Keys. It is not about noon, and we hear the cheering of our men, and in short time we get the news that Fremont is badly whipped. But while we are rejoicing over the victory, we have to mourn the loss of our noble and gallant cavalry general, Ashby, who fell in the beginning of the fight between our rear guard and Fremont's advance.

We spend the remainder of the day watching Shields, while our artillery is shelling them at long range. Night comes on and it is necessary to put out a large picket force, while the rest of the army bivouac for the night, for we all know that the morrow will bring us hard fighting again.

chapter fourteen

WOUNDED AT PORT REPUBLIC

At reveille, all is astir. Jackson soon puts us in motion, and our long column marches through the town of Port Republic, and across the South Fork of the Shenandoah, on wagons sunk in the stream, making an imperfect pontoon bridge. We lose much valuable time in crossing. We fall in line of battle as soon as we get over the river. We can see Ewell's division for some distance, which is coming from Cross Keys. We know that it will be some time before they can reach us, as they have to cross that same pontoon bridge over which we have just crossed.

The day is bright and beautiful, but very hot, and we are in one of the loveliest valleys I ever saw, but with cruel and powerful batteries frowning upon us. It is now evident, as has often been the case before, that the Stonewall brigade will have the heaviest part of the fighting to do. We are half a mile from the enemy's batteries, which occupy a hill, and this beautiful, level plain between us. Not a shot has yet been fired, except a few stray ones by our skirmishers. Just now it looks to us impossible for any of us to reach those batteries alive, with their powerful infantry force supporting them. We are ordered to advance, which we do steadily and in splendid order. We go but a short distance when the enemy opens fire on us, artillery and infantry combined. Grape-shot, being used by the artillerists, makes the situation appear more desperate, yet we keep on advancing rapidly, although it seems to us that nothing short of a miracle can preserve any of us alive. The fire continues so hot and destructive that the command wavers. Col. Grigsby rides in front of us saying in the most determined manner, "Those batteries must be taken." We reform our line and again face the deadly fire.

Ewell's men have crossed the river and have formed in line of battle, and now come forward at double quick to our support, but the heavy batteries still continue to pour such destructive fire of shot, canister, and grape on us, that no troops can sustain it, and we see the utter futility of the attempt. Just at this opportune moment, we hear the "Rebel yell," and we see on our right a Confederate brigade, Taylor's Louisianans, advancing from a woodland. Truly the darkest hour is just before day. At that instant I was struck by a grape-shot, and feel insensible. When I recovered consciousness, I raised myself up, and looking, saw my company a good distance in front of me. I find my arm dangles helpless by my side. My shoulder has been struck by the shot. It has torn my oil cloth, which we tied in triple folds, from my right shoulder to my left side. This is no doubt what saved my life. Physical strength fails me, and amid showers of striking shells, I retrace my steps to the rear. I see Sanford lying dead as I pass on.

In the rear, I find many wounded, and the enemy's shells are still flying around us, but they soon cease, and we know that the day is decided, and that the enemy is retreating. A surgeon came up and examined my shoulder. He says there are no bones broken, so I hope soon to regain the use of my arm, and decline going to the hospital, for which I have an even greater horror than for a battle field.

We hear that the Confederates have taken the Federal batteries, and Shields is badly whipped. His loss must be very great. Nearly every man in our regiment claims to have been struck by some kind of a missile, but most of them are not dangerously wounded. I am now excused from duty until I can use my arm.

Ewell's division follows the retreating Federals for many miles. Unable to give Shields any further assistance, Fremont is also retreating down the valley. Jackson has ordered his force at Cross Keys to fall back and burn the bridge, so Fremont was unable to cross the river. It now appears that Jackson is again in possession of his own. The army retires to a good camping ground in one of the gaps of the Blue Ridge, and rests quietly for four days.

This valley campaign has been in progress for little over a month, and has raised Jackson into the zenith of fame, and has given him a certain kind of precedence over every other officer in the southern army. The Confederates have implicit confidence in his ability, and the Northern army fears him more than any other thing in the South. We men in his old command are much gratified by his promotion to Lieutenant General. The high esteem in which he is held by both officers and men is unbounded. The great power and influence he wields over us is something wonderful. We moralize as to its cause. First, it is the implicit confidence we have in him as to his ability and sincerity. Then we love him because he cares for us, and shares our hardships and privations. Then there is the certain decisiveness about him which constitutes the commander. So when he tells us to march to the cannon's mouth, we know that he sees the necessity, and means for us to do what he says. And then, too, we know he is a praying man, and we believe there is a God who hears and answers prayers, and this gives us a faith in our general, which otherwise we could not have.

chapter fifteen

THE PRIVATE SOLDIER

Now while we have time to analyze and express our thoughts and feelings, I must say a few words in behalf of the part the private soldier takes in this tremendous struggle for liberty. In the first place, there are such vast numbers of them, all dressed alike, looking alike, and when in ranks, stepping alike, that they almost lose their identity (except when we get a furlough and go home), so that citizens and perhaps some connected with the army, get in the habit of thinking of the soldiers as a great big machine, made for the purpose of marching, fighting, and obeying orders, forgetting that the majority of them are brave, patriotic men, fighting conscientiously for what they believe to be right, willing to face danger and even death for what they believe to be their duty. The soldier reflects and realizes that "it is not all of death to die." It is often with quivering hearts that they advance steadily and with firm steps in the very mouth of the cannon, or rush unflinchingly to the bayonet charge. None but a good solider, one who never thinks, can appreciate the every day suffering from the cold and heat, the hunger and thirst, the anxiety and excitement, the watching and weariness on the march and in the camp. We do not complain, dear citizen reader, but we are very human and we want your sympathy and appreciation. You must know our needs before you can supply them. With a few exceptions, everywhere we have been, either marching or camping, the citizens have shown great thoughtfulness and kindness for the comfort of the "poor soldier" as they call him. As far as it is possible our field officers are considerate of our comfort and safety, but sometimes it is impossible for them to palliate the horrors of war for us. You must know, dear reader, that we do not march across the battle field, scale the enemy's breast works, or drive them before us, by thinking and caring for our own safety. Our officers know that we have to endure this exposure of our lives to drive the enemy from our fair Southern land.

Now as a matter of course, the history of this war will be written up by many able historians. All due renown will be given to the prominent commanders of the army. Their laurels will never wither. Their fame will increase with age, whilst little will be said or written about the private soldier. So I am going to refer to the remarkable bravery of some of my fellow soldiers, by naming a few of them.

Preeminent is Mike Foster, of the Monroe Guards, a company belonging to the 27th Regiment. Every battle in which we have been engaged, he has made himself conspicuous and actually distinguished, by his remarkable valor and courage. He is a kind hearted, genial fellow. We are all very much attached to him as a friend, as well as proud of him as a brave fellow soldier. And there is color bearer, Powell of the 27th, who is another uncommonly brave man, as well as our handsome captain, Phillip Frazier of Company E. George Harper of Company E is another one who deserves special mention for his valor and endurance. It is not my intention to disparage any of my other fellow soldiers by referring to these, for I believe there are many more who are just as truly brave as these I have mentioned, only not so demonstrative. One can be a good, faithful, honorable soldier, and yet be a timid man. A large number of soldiers belong to this class, and I feel much inclined to defend said class, for I belong to it myself. Yet I would die rather than shirk duty! But we cannot deny, that those possessing of great physical bravery, make a better show for bravery and efficiency. In fact, they infuse the rest of us to do and to dare. However, both classes deserve great credit, for duty so faithfully performed, and for danger so unflinchingly braved. It is a great comfort to us to remember that it is we men in ranks who execute the great strategic conceptions of our leaders, and we realize this burden of duty and honor.

Now that I am trying to set forth facts as they are, I might as well tell the whole truth, and that makes it necessary for me to speak of a third class. I am sorry to say that it is somewhat numerous. They are those who do not seem to feel any responsibility or obligation whatever to any person or any cause. To shirk duty and danger seems to be their object, and at the same time draw rations and a few clothes. But this class is to be found among citizens also. They always have been and always will. So the "poor soldier" who is so unfortunate as to belong to the third class is, we presume, no more contemptible in the army than he is in the daily walk of every day life. But war is a fire that tries men's soul and the baser alloy, is in a measure, separated by the crucial test.

chapter sixteen

SEVEN DAYS BATTLES

June, 1862. We continue to hear through scouts that the Federals under Fremont and Shields are retreating down the valley. We now hear that McClellan is threatening our Southern capitol with a hundred thousand men, and we have orders to prepare to march on the morrow to aid in the defense of Richmond.

June 14, 1862. We start on our march to join Gen. Lee's forces. We tramp along the country roads until we reach Gordonsville. At this point we get on the railroad and march on the track to Louisa Court House. The weariness of the march is here relieved by a ride on the cars to Hanover Junction. We now march across the country in the direction of Mechanicsville.

June 26th. Proceeded by the cavalry, we continue our march, and when within a few miles of Mechanicsville, we hear firing. In the evening, we hear that Gen. Lee has turned McClellan's right wing, and that the Federals have fallen back to Old Cold Harbor House, which is the enemy's main line of defense. We reach this place a little after the middle of the day, on the 27th.

Jackson immediately makes preparations to fight. We feel that this is an important epoch with the Confederacy. The whole force from the valley under Jackson, and great many other troops from the south, with the whole of Lee's army that has been guarding Richmond, are now united, making a tremendous body of men, and we are facing a hundred thousand men. We fear that there will be an awful loss of life in the great battles that are pending, and even begun. Lee is commander-in-chief of the Southern forces.

We find that A.P. Hill has recoiled before the enemy's breastworks. Immediately the veteran troops of Jackson are thrown forward, and the forest reverberates. The Federals occupy a strong position, a crest bristling with cannon and triple lines of breastworks, on the south side of the Chickahominy. There is a wide field that must be crossed before we can reach the hill they occupy. But the Stonewall Division is not immediately ordered into action, and we wait for some time protected by a wooded hill, while the rest of Jackson's corps are fighting hard in our front. Wounded Texans pass us going to the rear, and ask us why we are here so inactive while the enemy is ruining our men in front. We wonder ourselves why it is that we are not ordered forward, and think that there must be some mistake. We can see that a stubborn combat is going on, and the enemy does not give way. It is said that Jackson became greatly discouraged, thinking that the whole of his corps was engaged, and little progress made toward dislodging the enemy. When he asked where the Stonewall division was, and it was told him that it had not been brought into action, he answered very impatiently, "Bring them to the front and sweep the field with the bayonet." We are now ordered to support Gen. D.H. Hill, and are advanced at a bayonet charge. There is a destructive fire poured into our ranks as we cross the wide stretch in front of us. But the fire becomes less fatal as we near their artillery. It is aimed too high. The whole of Jackson's line swept forward in our wild bayonet charge. The "rebel yell" indicates our triumph as we take the crest and the artillery crowning it. This terminates the struggle. Those artillerists must have been ordered to stand to their guns until McClellan passed his army over the Chickahominy, for they stood there until almost the last one of them was killed.

But they had fired too high toward the last, so that very few of our men were struck with their shells, although we got within fifty yards of their cannons before they were silenced. As they belched forth their deadly missiles, mingled with the flashes of fire, it made a frightfully sublime and terrific show, for it is now dusk. The burning woods light up the scene. McClellan's army is now in full retreat. This is called the battle of Cold Harbor. It is the 27th of June, 1862.

Night of the 27th. McClellan's troops are in full retreat. He will find it slow work getting his troops over that swamp in the dark. The only way of egress is over narrow corduroy roads, and if horse or wagon gets off the poles, it means to be hopelessly swamped in.

The battle being over, we rest until morning. All night long we could hear the groans of the wounded Federals, and it sounded so piteous that I almost felt impelled to go to their assistance, but I know everything is much confused in our front. When morning comes, we follow up the enemy. We fired the bridges across the Chickahominy, and this detains us all day.

June 29th. Magruder is on front of us, and in the afternoon we can hear him fighting at Savage Station. We hear that the losses on both sides are heavy. Night comes on. The grey rest on the field, and the blue take up their retreat toward James River, leaving many prisoners in the hands of the grey.

June 30th. At dawn the advance of our corps is at Savage Station. Twenty-five thousand strong, we pass on toward White Oak Swamp, through thick woods, deep creeks, and small swamps. Deep woods appear in front of us, and the guide says, "White Oak Swamp. There is heavy cannonading on both sides, but we cannot cross as the bridge is burned. We can hear heavy firing in front of us and we learn that Longstreet and A.P. Hill are fighting furiously at Frazier's Farm. Our troops drive them from the field and they continue their retreat. The loss of life in these last two battles has been very great. As our division marches over these battle fields, the sights we see are heart rending. As we march over one place, we count sixty-eight dead bodies of the Federals, and they are close enough for anyone to step from one to the other. Most of them are shot directly in the stomach. This was only a small, a very small, portion of the dead, but it shows how great was the slaughter, and how sure the aim! All along the line of our march from Cold Harbor to Malvern Hill we come upon dead bodies on the road side and even in the road. The artillery wheels have passed over many of them. Horrible sight! The army is much worn out, and often detained by fighting in our front. While we are stopped we often fall asleep for a short time. Once, whilst dozing, Judge Fry, of Lewisburg, came along and called out, "Lieutenant Edgar." I started up, and he gave me a letter from my dear old home. This sweet breath of domestic affection revives me very much, and I take fresh courage.

The Federal army by this time seems very much demoralized. Our army takes many prisoners. We often meet squads of Federalists without guards, asking us the way to Richmond. This amuses us not a little. We valley men know as little of the direction to Richmond as they do. There is such a labyrinth of roads all through this country. But we know we are following the Yankee army, and it is trying to get to the shelter of its gunboats.

We reach Malvern Hill on the first day of July, 1862. We find the enemy occupying the hill, their position being very strong, hundreds of guns massed on the hill and behind them on the river from gunboats. The hill rises one hundred and fifty feet, woodland and swamps surrounding the base of the hill.

Late in the evening, our guns first open fire, and the Federals respond with terrific force, their gunboats throwing their great balls a long distance in our rear. I have just now seen a ball cut a large pine tree off, the upper part turning top down as it strikes the ground. The infantry fire has not yet been so heavy, but the roar of the cannons is fearful. Our center, Rodes' Brigade, now charges and is repulsed with great loss. It begins to grow dark with the smoke of the guns, and our whole line is ordered to charge. The order is only partially understood, perhaps not delivered. We who do go forward, thinking we are supported, after going over a small knoll, find to our horror that the other troops are not with us, and it is growing so dark from the smoke. We are now exposed to the fire from our own men as well as from the enemy. Our situation is perilous, indeed, and for a short while we feel there is no hope for our lives. We lie down at once, as it would be folly to turn back or go forward.

There always seems to be men for the most trying emergencies. Some brave fellows volunteered to crawl back and report our situation to our commander, so we get back without being fired upon by the grey.

The fighting continues furiously. The sun goes down. Jackson throws us forward again, but Magruder's troops bear the brunt of the last fighting. Night comes on and the fighting ceases. Our loss is fearful. Our dead lay in swathes, as if cut down by a scythe. Our brave Colonel Grigsby has been shot through the body by a "Minnie-ball," but he refused to get off of his horse, making one of the men from the 27th get up behind him, and hold him on, saying he was going thus to Richmond. But Dr. McGuire said he was pretty limber when he got back to the field hospital. We feel anxious about him, and hope his wound may not prove fatal. This battle is not a victory for either side. Our loss must be greater than the Yankees. We men in ranks think it a fruitless battle, and a dreadful waste of human life. This makes seven days of fighting around Richmond. The battles are spoken of as Chickahominy, Gaine's Mill (or Cold Harbor), Garnet's and Golding's farms, Peach Orchard, Savage Station, White Oak Swamp, Frazier's Farm, and Malvern Hill. Our division has only been actively engaged in the one at Cold Harbor and Malvern Hill. We retire a short distance from the battle field. Our rations are cooked and sent to us. We lie down and sleep until morning.

Morning. When we get up and commence to move around all feel such an unusual apathy, such a lack of energy, that someone says, "What is the matter with us all, any how?" "Has this fight put an end to our energy?" Another one answers, "Maybe it has. I have just now heard that 'Old Jack's' staff of officers can't get him up this morning." A third one answers him, "Yes, they did get him to move enough to say, 'do let me sleep this morning, there will be no enemy here this morning, they are just as willing to rest as we are.'" Now we all wonder if Jackson has lost his energy and we actually feel concerned about him. So much so, that our interest in him rouses our lagging energies. It is the first time that we have ever heard anything akin to Stonewall Jackson's showing any inclination to rest himself when anything in the shape of duty could possibly claim his attention. However, judging "the future by the past" we conclude that Old Jack knows what he is talking about, even if he was asleep, when he said "there will be no enemy here this morning," and we rest content, hoping that Gen. McClellan and his army are as sleepy as we are. It has rained during the night, and we are somewhat damp, but the sun comes out and we dry ourselves without trouble. We find that during the night McClellan has been withdrawing his troops to Harrison's Landing, under cover of his gunboats, and we are more than satisfied to rest for awhile, for our troops are very much broken down and scattered. If now we were suddenly called out to fight we might, literally speaking, be caught napping. We retire in the direction of Richmond and go into camp for a week or ten days.

chapter seventeen

BATTLE OF CEDAR MOUNTAIN

Now to give a true reminiscence of the life of a brave and faithful soldier. Telling the whole truth it becomes necessary to make a note of something that may offend the sensibilities of the exquisitely refined. Of such I beg pardon, but "my path takes me directly over that line," and I see no way around it. It is the lice that beset us so mercilessly. As the war advances and large bodies of men congregate at the centers of activity, men sleep in their clothing, very rarely having a change. So the body lice seems to be a natural and unavoidable consequence. But do not get the idea we are ashamed of them. On the contrary, we are proud of them. (I only apologize to the exceedingly refined). We think these pesky things are a more convincing evidence of a faithful soldier than brass buttons. For it is only those who stay in camp and are always at the post of duty, that are worse beset with them on their persons. The boys who are constantly running home and getting excused from duty, have very few of them as a rule. These lice are a constant reminder to us, even in our sleep. It is scarcely possible that Pharaoh and his subjects could have felt the severity of lice any more actually than we American soldiers and possibly less. As I remember, it was only the frogs that the Egyptians could not keep out of their kneading pans, but I think it is some doubtful about where these vermin wander. At any rate, we cannot inspect too closely. We may bathe our bodies, wash our clothes, and kill all the miserable little vermin that we can find, but it is of no avail. The very ground on which we walk and sleep seems alive with them. The Rebels blame the Yankees with introducing this intolerable nuisance, for we never had so much trouble with them until we got to camping where the Federals had been and using supplies which we captured from them. We imagine the largest and thriftiest lice we see have U.S. on their backs.

We have been resting quietly in camp for more than a week. We have just heard the Gen. McClellan has been superseded in command by General Pope, and it now becomes evident that the Federals have abandoned for the present the route to Richmond by the James. We hear that large forces of Federals are coming into Virginia by Manassas again. Between the 10th and the 15th of July we are ordered into the city to take trains for Gordonsville. As we march through the streets of Richmond, the citizens all come out to "see Jackson's men." They imagine them to be more than common mortals, so great have been their reputation for valor and thrilling adventures. I think the boys and ladies are somewhat disappointed when they find us looking so much like the rest of humanity. We have to wait here two or three hours, but we do not tire, for it is possible for us to buy all we want to eat. The restaurants are well supplied, and we have just been "paid off," so we put in our time quite agreeably. I, for one, bought four medium sized apple pies, and tell it not, dear friend, I ate three and gave the fourth away. They were the only pies I have had since entering the army, except whilst I was at home on furlough.

Train time comes and we are off to Gordonsville. On reaching that point, we march to the neighborhood of Orange Court House. The Stonewall Brigade is in front. Here we go into camp. Pope is in front of us with over forty-five thousand troops. We are reinforced by A.P. Hill. On the 6th of August Pope crosses the Rappanhannock, and on the 7th we break camp and begin to move to meet him. We have enjoyed our rest here very much after our experiences around Richmond. As usual before great battles our commanders have much maneuvering to do, as it is impossible to tell when and where the enemy will strike. We are within a few miles of Cedar Mountain, a point to which we know the Yankees are advancing. As we march along we are much annoyed by the cavalry passing us, and we complain of their impertinence.

This is the 9th of August and is the hottest day I ever experienced. Many of our men have fallen out of ranks because of the intense heat. Just now we were resting by the roadside with our guns stacked, when to our amazement someone rides up and asks for "the bloody 27th," and we recognize our brave Col. Grigsby. We cheer wildly. He greets us most cordially. You will remember he was shot through the body at Malvern Hill less than six weeks ago, and is now back to take command of his regiment again. What a brave, determined soldier he is. Few men would have returned so soon after being so seriously wounded. We reach Cedar Mountain about three o'clock and are rapidly formed in line of battle, with our guns loaded, ready for the conflict.

The battle opens as usual with terrific cannonading on both sides. In front of us are a part of Carpenter's and Rockbridge batteries. Many men are being killed by the enemy's shells. Our brigadier-general is killed by one of the shells, and the brigade is now led by the gallant Col. Ronald. We are anxiously concerned at this time with what is occurring on our right as we greatly fear Gen. Ewell will be forced back, but we are quickly relieved by hearing the "Rebel yell," which is a signal for us to go forward. We advance, loading and firing with great rapidity, and we soon come in close quarters with the enemy. Just here we discover a strong Federal force on our left flank. Our line begins to waver, and we fall back fifty yards or more. At this critical moment, Stonewall Jackson gallops up to us in a most excited manner and draws his sword. I am within ten feet of him and see and hear him distinctly. He shouted, "Rally brave men. Rally and follow me. Jackson will lead you." We rallied and pressed forward. Our line was soon restored. Jackson rode along the front and shouted, "Give them the bayonet! Give them the bayonet! Forward and drive them!" We marched rapidly forward. Soon afterwards we ran into a lot of Federal prisoners, who I suppose were captured by one of the brigades on our front, which came up just in our time of dire need. Someone called out to General Jackson, "What must be done with these prisoners?" And his reply is, "Turn them loose and follow me forward on the enemy." This we do with all of our old ardor, and the Blue line gives way at once. It is drawing towards night and the firing soon ceases. A grand victory for us, but we did advance only a small ways. In this fight we lose one of our best and bravest men in Company E, John Church. His bravery and faithfulness to duty deserve to be specially recognized.

We encamp on the Federal side of the battle field. After we get our supplies, four of us, Orderly Sergeant Davis, Sergeant Patton, Color bearer Powell of our regiment, and myself, conclude we will reconnoiter the battle ground, expecting to find almost anything but live Yankees. Curiosity leads us further than discretion dictates. Patton becomes much interested in a nice medicine case. I, in two fine horses that were rambling about. Powell brings up the rear with some trophy or other while Davis goes with his gun a short distance in front of us, it being the only loaded one in our crowd. Very unexpectedly our surrender is demanded by a Yankee picket force. Davis promptly answers, "You are the men to surrender. You are our prisoner. Throw down your arms." Now to say this on the spur of the moment requires more presence of mind and pluck than I think I could have, knowing that there are only four of us in the crowd, and only one loaded gun. However we all take in the situation at once. I call out, "Come up, boys, all of you, quick, we have some prisoners." Patton leaves his surgical case, Powell leaves his treasure, I my horse, and we all go to Davis' support and stand there while thirteen meek looking Yankees walk out of a woodland and march before us into camp. When we reach there and the prisoners see only four of us with two guns, and only one of them loaded, they are much chagrined. It is not strange that they would be deceived, as the moon gave a dim light, and the men were raw recruits, having only entered the army two months ago, and they do not seem to be over enthusiastic in their cause. It is very evident that those men will never again lose sight of discretion.

Jackson followed the Federals a few miles, but finding a strong reserve withdraws and falls back near Gordonsville. In a few days, General Lee, with a large part of his army, joins us here. We wonder why now the Confederates do not attack Gen. Pope and upon inquiring, find our cavalry is not with us, that Gen. Stuart is raiding.

We make an advance on the 20th, but find nothing but the rear guard, and that Pope and his army have crossed the Rappahanock. We now hear of Gen. Jeb. Stuart making a bold dash on the rear of the Federal army, reaching headquarters and nearly capturing Gen. Pope himself. Stuart captured some valuable papers containing important information. We soon hear that Lee wants Jackson to get around to Pope's rear, and has ordered him to move on.

August 25th. We commence our march today, going north. We understand that Jackson desires a forced march with guns loaded, an unusual precaution. We march twenty-five miles today, and are much worn out. Our rations are very meager, and we eat them with roasting ears and green apples. We camp near Salem. As we draw near our camping place for the night, we see Jackson standing near the roadside with his cap under his arm. He always takes his cap off when his men are passing. Forgetting how tired we are, we begin to cheer. He instantly checks us with a wave of his hand. This we understand is a signal to be quiet, and we pass silently along. But as we pass we catch inspiration from the noble mien of our commander. Jackson, turning to his staff, was heard to say, "Who could not conquer with such troops as these?"

We understand now that Jackson is making a flank movement, and wants to conceal his whereabouts from the enemy.

August 26th. We turn east and pass through the Bull Run Mountains at Thoroughfare Gap, and proceed by another hard day's march to Bristoe Station on the Orange railroad. Stuart's cavalry joins us at Gainesville and guards our right flank, and at the same time watches the main army of Pope about Warrington. When we reached Bristoe Station, we captured a railroad train going east, but it proved to contain nothing of any value. Our corps has now marched fifty miles in the last two days and we have no supplies and are depending on what we may capture from the enemy. General Pope's army supplies are at Manassas Junction, four miles from here. General Trimble volunteers to take the 21st North Carolina and the 21st Georgia regiments on there this night, and capture those stores. Jackson accepts the offer and they promptly proceed in the darkness to make this hazardous attempt. Later we hear they have succeeded.

chapter eighteen

SECOND BATTLE OF MANASSAS

August 27th. General Jackson with most of his army leaves Bristoe Station for Manassas Junction. Ewell's division is left here to watch for the approach of Pope and to impede him as much as possible, but if pressed too hard to retire to Jackson at Manassas.

In the afternoon large forces of Yankees were seen coming from the direction of Warrenton. Some Louisiana regiments and one Georgia regiment were drawn up to receive them. Two columns of the enemy advanced against them, but soon broke and fled in confusion. With fresh columns coming up, it soon became evident that Pope's main force was near. Gen. Ewell gave the order to retire toward Manassas and there join Gen. Jackson. This we do in good order, without the capture of a single man. When we get to Manassas we find our men have captured large stores of many things we need, also three hundred prisoners, eight field pieces, two hundred and fifty horses, besides two miles of box cars loaded with army supplies and even luxuries. We regale ourselves with all of these good things.

I find some fruit preserves that I very much enjoy and appropriate any thing that I need. Our horse's backs are packed with two or three day's rations and our wagons are loaded with all that they can haul. Then our men fire the enemy's stores. We retire this night from Manassas Junction in the direction of Bull Run. It is nearly dark but I recognize the ground as being near the old battle field of Manassas. One of the first objects that my eyes rest on is Stonewall Jackson lying on the ground, fast asleep, with his staff of officers around him, some of them asleep, others sitting on their blankets. We bivouac near them. The next morning, the 28th of August, officers and men astir early. As the day grows the place looks more familiar, and we wonder, is there going to be another battle on this already historical spot? The enemy is evidently preparing to give battle. They greatly outnumber us, and are between us and Gen. Lee and Longstreet's Corps. But nothing daunted, Jackson proceeds to prepare for an attack. He knows by taking the initiative he can choose his ground for the attack. He disposes his troops one or two miles from the Warrenton Turnpike and nearly parallel with it. Ewell occupies the center, A.P. Hill the left, and Taliaferro the right. This disposition of his forces had barely been completed when the Federalists were found to be advancing in heavy masses along the Warrenton Pike. A portion of Taliaferro's Division began to skirmish with the front of the Federal column. The rest of his division and our division were marshaled to attack the enemy. Jackson now threw forward his line so determinedly as to make the enemy take a stand. It is now afternoon, about two-thirty. Our batteries are now advancing to a hill, where they deliver an effective fire upon the Federalists who reply with their guns. Our artillery is then promptly moved to another position, from which we enfilade the enemy's guns. Our infantry is again pressed forward and the struggle begins in all its fury. We occupy an open field and receive and return the volleys of our enemy's at a distance of three hundred yards. We stubbornly contest this ground until dark, when the enemy suddenly retires and we are left masters of the field. This has been a bloody engagement with many casualties. Among others our division commander, Gen. Ewell, has been shot in the knee, and will lose his leg. We are anxiously looking for Longstreet to reinforce us. His corps is expected through Thoroughfare Gap, and we hope he is following our route. Our commander-in-chief, Gen. Lee, is with them.

Morning of the 29th. Anxiously do we watch the distant road from the Thoroughfare Gap. We are impatient for Longstreet's arrival. Jackson's Corps is confronted by the whole Federal army, and it is trying to force us back from Bull Run, and crush us before our friends arrive. Jackson has disposed us along an unfinished railroad, and it makes a good fortification. About the middle of the forenoon the cannonading begins. As the day advances we see clouds arising in the direction of Thoroughfare Gap, and soon Stewart's couriers come with the glad news that Longstreet is advancing. Jackson has arranged his infantry in two lines of battle with our artillery in the rear.

2 p.m. Pope began to attack with his infantry with great fury. Especially does our left suffer. This is occupied with A.P. Hill's division. The enemy rushes forward in obstinate assault only to be mowed down and to recoil in confusion. Time and again they do this. At many places along the line the fighting is in close quarters, especially with a brigade of Louisianans, who resort to throwing stones, using their bayonets and fighting with the butts of their guns, their ammunition being exhausted, and now has to be brought to them by brave volunteers. Our division has not been brought into action but has been kept in reserve and we are exposed to a heavy artillery fire. At one time I had been resting against a small crooked tree, and with out any mental exercise whatever, took a step or two from the tree, when it was struck by a piece of shell passing down its side, and driving into the ground four or five inches. With a shudder I looked at that deadly missile and saw how near I came to being killed. I felt that a special Providence had kept me from a horrible death and that a merciful God is still sparing my life while so many others are being hurled into Eternity. As the day grows older we are brought into action. The enemy did not move against the center as stolidly as against the left wing. Night comes on and stops this bloody fray. Men are detailed to cook rations, and bring them to us. We still occupy the railroad cut but move back a pace to lie down on our arms. We leave a double picket force.

August 30th. The forenoon is spent in a desultory cannonading directed to first one and then another part of our lines. Meantime, the enemy is disposing of his troops under cover of the woods and hills. They are massed chiefly in front of Jackson. Longstreet occupies the right wing of the army. General Jackson's ranks are fearfully thinned by the last two days fighting. Yet he stoutly holds his ground, although in some of the commands, one third of the men are gone, killed, wounded and missing. Nevertheless those who are left have lost none of their valor. By the middle of the afternoon the enemy makes a show of an attack along the lines of Longstreet. But soon without preliminary skirmishing, they advance in enormous masses against Jackson's front. Three lines of battle roll up against the Confederates, the enemy showing a dogged determination to break through our ranks by sheer force of number. The Confederates exhausting their ammunition again resort to throwing stones to beat back their enemies. When Jackson's troops began to weary of the combat he sent word to Longstreet to move to his relief. The Confederate artillery was advanced and showered a crushing fire upon the enemy. Longstreet forms his lines back of us, but they soon appear in open field, Longstreet taking the front. The lines of battle sweep forward, exhibiting the most magnificent military display that I have ever seen since the war began. We move forward and the enemy is driven from hilltop to hilltop. They retreat in some order and endeavor to make a stand at different points. But they at last gave way and fall back, and the sound of the battle dies away. The Confederates follow until it is too dark to distinguish friends from foe. We lie down to rest upon the ground we have won. As we pressed forward over the ground occupied by the Federals during the battle, I never saw half as many dead men at one time since I have been in the army, and the loss on our side has been very heavy. Of course now we can only conjecture, but it must sum up into many hundreds. This we do know, that it has been a great victory for the South. Some might say as great as the first Manassas, but the two can scarcely be compared, there being more than three times as many men engaged in this than there was in the first Manassas, and this did not result in a rout exactly to the Federals. Although badly whipped, they retreated with some order. This night we are allowed to lie down on our oilcloths, which is a restful change from our arms. On the morning of the 31st we arise from our sleep with the sun pouring down. We are tired, shivering and utterly comfortless. The world never looked so gloomy. But we proceed to get our breakfast, and warm and dry ourselves by the camp fires. Jackson's Corps soon receive orders to march in the direction of Centerville. We now hear that Pope, largely reinforced by troops from McClellan, has made a stand at this place. We hear that Gen. Jackson has orders to turn his position and make him retreat, if possible without a battle. So we are marched hurriedly over rough, round-about country roads, until the next day when we land in the rear of Centerville. This takes the enemy by surprise (just as Old Jack intended it to) and they at once resume their retreat, but when they reach Fairfax Courthouse they find Jackson ready to strike their line of march from the side. The Yankees here make a stand and draw up their troops on a small ridge and offer to give battle. Jackson threw his infantry into line and advanced against the enemy. Just at this point we have a sharp and bloody little battle. At one time they broke through our lines, and for a short time we feared they might overpower us by superiority of numbers, but our line is soon reestablished. The Federals fight furiously and with stubborn will. All at once the tide turns in our favor and the enemy falls back and the battle dies away as suddenly as it began. A storm of lightening and thunder came up while the engagement was going on, and we had the disadvantage of the rain beating in our faces. The enemy retires in the darkness. This is called the battle of Ox Hill, and was fought on the first of September. Amid the storm and darkness we seek for some place to camp that will afford us any shelter and comfort and we "turn in" for the night. We are much worn out with marching and fighting and the storm adds to our discomfort.

September 2nd. The weather is more favorable this morning and we are allowed to rest all day. We now hear the reports of the continuous battles of the last week. It has been a costly sacrifice of human life to the Confederates. The total loss in these different engagements has been seven thousand, five hundred, of whom eleven hundred were killed. Of this loss Jackson lost nearly five thousand, eight hundred and five killed. This great loss in his command was owing to the fact that his corps was always in advance and received the brunt of the attack. We have captured over seven thousand prisoners, besides many army stores, and have driven the enemy from northern Virginia. Jackson's Corps thinks that the credit of all these victories belongs more to Jackson than to any of the other commanders. His troops always took the advance and brunt of the battle. The celerity of his marches, the promptness of his action in capturing the Junction, and the bravery with which he held it until Longstreet's arrival, all showed what a wonderful general he is, and how much he contributed to the victory we gained. During these forced marches we rarely see our supply wagons, and at one time I had to wear my shirt five weeks without being laundered.

In the evening of the second we have orders to start in the morning in the direction of the Potomac. We cook our day's rations and early on the morning of the third, we start out. We march very cautiously as the enemy may show unexpectedly at some point. They certainly gave up at Ox Hill with stubborn resistance, and it behooves us to watch with vigilance. This day we march as far as Dranesville. The fourth brings us to Leesburg, and we arrive at the Potomac without adventure or annoyance from the enemy.

chapter nineteen

"Maryland, My Maryland"

By this time a large portion of the Federal army is north of the Potomac. On the morning of the 5th of September, Jackson's command has arrived on the south bank, and we cross over at White's Ford. We understand that there is to be a Maryland campaign. We crossed the river without serious difficulty, the water not over waist deep. I took off my shoes. The pebbles cut my feet and hurt me so acutely that I almost felt like giving up and sitting down. I made a mental resolution that however many times I should have to wade the Potomac thereafter, I'll never take off my shoes again. The ford here is about a half a mile wide and it takes a large body of men a long while to cross over, but we are over now and are filled with the highest glee and enthusiasm. As line after line reaches the Maryland shore, we rend the air with cheers, the bands playing "Maryland, My Maryland." Our army is in fine health and spirits.

The first order we get is to break the locks of the canal, so as to drain out the water and make it unnavigable. On the 6th we occupy the Baltimore and Ohio Railroad. We find many

Southern sympathizers. We have the most stringent orders against straggling or depredations on private property, but as I am almost without shoes,

I ask permission of Col. Grisby to be allowed to go ahead of the army and do some shopping, but he says it will be directly against orders for him to give me permission and that he is obligated to refuse. Now I cannot march barefooted when there are shoe stores in reach, so I must "maneuver" some. I have a friend, Lieutenant Yarrell of Wheeling, who is in need of some clothing, too, and he agrees to go with me. So by fast walking and flanking we get in advance of the command and reach Frederick City in time to do some shopping without attacking notice sufficient to call down discipline for disobeying orders. Our conscience does not upbraid us one bit, for we know we are just as free from a desire to be lawless or ungentlemanly with the citizens as Col. Grisby, or even as Gen. Jackson himself might be. Our bodies feel much more comfortable for the clothing we procured, and paid for, too. However, we do not expect to tell the other boys what we have done or encourage them to do likewise for many would take advantage of getting out of ranks and get boisterous. So we intend to keep quiet about our little "flank movement."

The army soon comes up and we rest at this place for four days. We are only too glad to do this for we have been doing some hard marching for the last few weeks. We are well fed here and enjoy the beautiful and highly cultivated country around to the fullest extent. The temptation to stroll a little is so great that one day two or three of us go as far as Boonsboro, a little village five or six miles distant, and barely escape being captured by a squad of Federal cavalry that dashed into the town while we were there. In order to avoid them we ran into a dwelling house. Fortunately for us the "lady of the manor" seemed to be a most refined and kind hearted person. She showed us the way to her garret and told us to stay there until the Federals should leave. At the same time she said she was a Union woman and thought that we were on the wrong side and would have to suffer for our rebellion. But she also said that she was sorry for the soldiers on both sides, and when opportunity offered would do all she could to save them from danger and suffering. As soon as it was safe she called us down, showed us the way out, and bade us God-speed. We thanked her sincerely and told her we wished her well, with a mental reservation that we hoped her side would not be on top at the close of the war. The Maryland people that I have seen are noble and generous. Many of them willing to fight for the South if they could.

It is now the 10th of September and we leave Frederick City, passing by Middletown, Boonsboro, and Williamsport and recrossing the Potomac River on our way to Harper's Ferry. The object in view is to capture the Federal force that is holding that place, where we arrive on the 12th and find the Federals on Bolivar Heights. Gen. Lee, in order to make sure of their capture, sends one division to the Maryland Heights, so the Federals are completely surrounded. Our batteries open on them simultaneously and they are able to make little resistance. After a furious cannonading from our batteries that only lasts an hour or a little more, the garrison surrenders with eleven thousand men, fifty or sixty pieces of artillery, not less than ten thousand stand of small arms, a great number of horses and wagons and stores of all. The garrison is treated with the most liberal terms. The officers are permitted to retain their side arms and all their personal effects upon their parole and the privates after being disarmed are also paroled. This occurs on the morning of September 15, 1862.

We are at once ordered from this place on a forced march to Sharpsburg. The thrilling news having been sent to Gen. Jackson that McClellan, with his grand army, had occupied Frederick City the day after Gen. Lee evacuated. He is now moving forward in pursuit of the Confederates, having in some way become cognizant of Lee's plans. He directs his whole force, with Sharpsburg being the objective point, to concentrate while Lee is scattered and before he can get it pulled together. We must get there as soon as possible, for Gen. Lee, we hear, is retreating. I do not know the distance, but this I do know. The physical effort required is greater than most of the men are equal to. So many of them are without shoes and are foot sore. But we start out in good spirits, confident that we are doing our duty and are marching to victory, for Stonewall Jackson is leading us. Night comes on and we have made as much as twenty miles or more. All of us are very tired and some have fallen out of rank, and many others are weary and footsore, that it seems that they will not be able to get much farther. So we bivouac for the night.

On the morning of the 16th we make an early start. I congratulate myself that I succeeded in getting my shoes whilst in Frederick City, otherwise I might now be among the number who have to fall out of ranks, and that is something I have never had to do yet. But soon we reach the Potomac, which we wade, this bringing us within two or three miles of Sharpsburg. Here we stop to rest for a short time, for we are thoroughly tired out. Two-thirds, if not more, of our men are straggling. Not from desire on the most part of them to shirk duty, but because of extreme fatigue that nature had to succumb to. Of course, some men will take advantage of circumstances to fall behind to keep out of the fight which is coming on.

chapter twenty

BATTLE OF SHARPSBURG

When we arrive on the battle field, we find there has been some heavy fighting. Generals Longstreet and D.H. Hill have had a hot engagement on the 14th. I have never before seen Jackson's Corps in such a depleted condition, but we are at once ordered to a position of great exposure and fearful danger, in support of Gen. Hood's left. The battle continues until late in the night, but the Confederates hold their ground and both armies sleep on their arms.

Very early on the morning of the 17th the battle opens again, furiously, with a terrific artillery fire which continues a long time from the Federal side, their tremendous shells frequently exploding half a mile in our rear over our wagon trains. The fighting is of the most stubborn and heroic nature. The heaviest fire falling upon Jackson's Corps, as we still hold the Confederate left. The enemy continually brings up fresh infantry support in great numbers. But we toil on against the overwhelming odds for several hours without the slightest cessation of violence. Our line is getting fearfully thinned under the dreadful fire. Many of our field officers have been killed and wounded. Still we fight on with the most stubborn valor, sometimes even breaking the ranks of the enemy, but only to be forced back again by the overwhelming numbers. Often during this long and terrible battle, I lose all hope of victory, and say to my comrades that we cannot hold out any longer, and that we will be compelled to give away, because of the fearfully increasing odds against us.

Yet we do continue to hold our ground with tenacity until Generals Hood and Early come up and take the front again, relieving us to some extent. They rush forward against the enemy with great fury, arresting their progress and after a few hours drive them back, and our lines are reestablished. This revives our fainting hopes of victory. Just at a critical moment, Gen. McLaws with his division, arrives on the field of battle and actually repulses the exultant enemy. Their lines begin to waiver and they retreat at least a half a mile with great loss, and their infantry is withdrawn. However, their artillery keeps up a terrific fire for the rest of the day. During the after part of the day, Jackson's men have a more sheltered position and do not suffer such severe loss. The Federals now return and attack the Confederates right and center, but are again repulsed. They discover that one of the brigades had been withdrawn to another part of the field, and they take advantage of this opportunity to press through into the Confederate lines and are only arrested by Gen. D.H. Hill and other officers rallying the remnants of several scattered brigades and a few pieces of artillery. The infantry, having little but their bayonets to depend upon, many of the men having fired every cartridge, present a bold front until two other batteries come up to their assistance. After a most desperate encounter that lasts an hour or more, the Yankees again retire. The Confederates make a most stubborn defense of the bridge over Antietam Creek, but it is at last gained by the Federals who cross over in great numbers and attack Longstreet's right, which commands the approaches. A.P. Hill's timely arrival with his division from Harper's Ferry is all that prevents the enemy from getting possession of the road that leads from Sharpsburg to the Potomac. After crossing the bridge the enemy dash forward and capture a battery, but they are cheated by Hill's batteries and others in different positions firing on them, they are driven back across the creek and the

Confederates retake the lost battery. Now the shades of night come on and for a time puts a stop to the bloody conflict. After all of the ups and downs of this awful day, the wavering first on one side and then on the other, as far as we men in ranks can judge, we can't see victory for either side. Each army holds about the same position it occupied this morning. The Federals greatly outnumber the Confederates. The number of souls from both sides that have gone to judgment and the still greater number of suffering and dying men left around us is a most solemn reflection for us who have escaped with unscathed bodies. We ask ourselves, "why are we still spared?" The Stonewall Brigade only numbers seventy-eight men. I have just assisted in counting them. Company E, my company, started in this morning with four members, and comes out tonight with two. I am only a second lieutenant and have had command of the brigade for two hours. Our rations are cooked by men detailed for that purpose and brought to us.

This morning, the 18th, all of us who are here feel ready to fight, but neither side makes any demonstration. The stragglers and broken down men keep coming in all day, and swell our ranks to a respectable number again. The greater part of the day is spent in burying our dead and removing the wounded. Late in the afternoon we recross the Potomac. We bring up the rear, Gen. Hill's corps having preceded us and guarding us while we cross. Stonewall Jackson, sitting on his horse in mid-stream, waits until the last one of us has passed over, and then he too passes over and joins his troops.

While this battle is claimed as a victory by the Federals, it reflects great credit on the Confederates for their valor and perseverance in fighting against such a great superiority of numbers. We now march three or four miles from the river and go into camp. Gen. Pendleton, on an elevation overlooking the river, is stationed to prevent the enemy from surprising us.

chapter twenty-one

IN VIRGINIA AGAIN

After being comfortably settled and soundly asleep in camp for two or three hours, we are partially aroused by hearing heavy firing of artillery and small arms combined, in the direction of the Potomac. But we are so thoroughly tired out that we take but little note of it and in a few minutes are sound asleep again. We know nothing of what is going on until morning. Then, however, the thrilling news reaches us, that the courageous A.P. Hill with his corps had a desperate night engagement with the Federals at Boteler's Ford which ended in a brilliant success for the Confederacy. The brief of the circumstances being as follows: as I have already said, while we were crossing the Potomac, Gen. Pendleton with his artillery was stationed on an eminence overlooking the river to prevent the Federals from crossing in pursuit of us. However, they advanced and placed heavy batteries upon the opposite bank. During the night a detachment crossed over above the batteries of Pendleton and completely surprised the Confederates and captured four of their guns. The others were removed to escape capture.

General Pendleton reported the disaster at midnight to Jackson and Lee. This caused great excitement with Jackson, more than he had ever been known to exhibit since the beginning of the war. And he immediately gave orders for the retaking of the guns. He actually started by himself in the direction of Boteler's Ford, which is just below where Pendleton occupies, giving orders for his troops to follow him without delay. That is the divisions of A.P. Hill, Early, and D.H. Hill. Lee's couriers found Jackson far in advance of his troops examining the position of the enemy. When Gen. Hill arrived on the ground, he spread out his division in two lines and made a vigorous charge on the enemy, notwithstanding the severe fire of shot and shell from their artillery across the river. The enemy made a stubborn resistance by bearing heavily down against Hill's left. But Hill rallied his whole force and made a second charge, forcing the enemy into the river and continuing to fire on them until it is claimed that few of them reached the northern bank of the river. In this engagement the Confederates fought entirely without artillery. They had to depend altogether on the musket and bayonet. This affair has caused much excitement among us soldiers today. It surely exhibits a wonderful amount of bravery and determination in all who were engaged in it. It is known as the Combat of Boteler's Ford.

Here ends these three wonderful campaigns that had continued for more than four months: the Valley Campaign, the Richmond Campaign and the Maryland Campaign. I have taken part in them all. I want to here give my opinion on the subject as to what I believe to be the honest truth. I hope not to become tiresome, for citizens cannot be in as full sympathy with the feelings of a good soldier as that fraternity can be with each other. But I am going to say this much, that the unflinching bravery, endurance, self-denial and sacrifice of personal comfort, practiced by both officers and men and their promptness to perform duty at any risk of life, cannot be surpassed in any army and will surely claim the admiration of all who know anything about it. At one time we did not see our baggage wagon for five weeks and during all that time I had no change of underclothing or opportunity to wash what I had on. Many of my acquaintances were enduring the same discomfort and not only in the way of clothing, but in every other imaginable way. We suffered marching and fighting when hungry. Many almost starved not having time to cook and eat even when the provision wagons were up with us. Yet we pressed bravely on without complaint, never allowing ourselves to get despondent or to shirk duty. Our brave and noble leader, Stonewall Jackson, was always with us. He endured almost as many privations as the common soldiers. This, of course, increased our admiration and affection for him as a man, and gave us more confidence, if possible, in him as a military commander. His influence over his men is something wonderful, moral as well as physical. While he so bravely leads us on as soldiers of the Confederacy, he, by his example, manifests his humble faith in God, and daily testifies that he is himself a "soldier of the cross." Anyone that stops to reflect at all on the important subject of God's infinite power and man's responsibility cannot help thinking that the kind of religion Stonewall Jackson professes, is worth all the effort it requires to practice it, even if the benefits reach no further than this world.

We now march some twenty or thirty miles into Virginia from the Potomac and camp here for several weeks. There seems to be a cessation of hostilities. The Federals as well as the Confederates seem to be willing to rest for a while. We are now enjoying this much needed rest and freedom from anxiety to the utmost extent. We have plenty to eat and opportunity to procure new clothes and wash our soiled ones. There is no strict military discipline or drill. Our commanders, of course, are keeping watch on the enemy's movements, but we soldiers in rank never see a Yankee or hear a gun fire. Truly we feel as though we have arrived at that point of human felicity called "Peace and Plenty." It is a wonderful transition compared with our experiences since last spring. We now, too, have the satisfaction of writing and receiving letters from our home folks, and this affords me greater pleasure than anything I can ask, except to go home. It is now about the 10th of October and we hear that Jackson has been promoted to Lieutenant-General. This gives us great satisfaction. Our division will now be led by Gen. Taliaferro.

18th of October. We are marched in the direction of the Potomac. We hear we are to destroy, as far as possible, the

Baltimore and Ohio Railroad. This great thoroughfare is of great use to the Federal government in transporting supplies to their army. General Jackson accompanied us. We burn all the bridges, break up the culverts, rip the nails from the cross ties, gather the ties into heaps, lay the iron rails across them and set fire to the whole. The heat of the burning ties warps the iron rails into every shape. We tear this road up for about thirty miles. This is the first work I ever did on a railroad.

Later in the month the Federals are beginning to make some demonstrations in the Valley and Jackson's corps is ordered there. We go part of the way by rail. We are all glad to get back to the beautiful valley. We go into quarters four miles below Winchester at Camp Harmon, our old camping ground of '61, November. We now hear that McClellan has been relieved of his command and General Burnside has been made his successor. Well, we now look for the new commander to soon try his fighting talent on us "poor Johnny Rebs."

I have been promoted to 1st Lieutenant, caused by the promotion of Lieutenant A.C. Snyder to regimental commissary. I have been in command of Company E fully half of the time since the Seven Days' fighting around Richmond, Captain Frazer having been seriously wounded in one of those battles. He has not yet returned to the army, and Lieut. Snyder is very frequently absent. This leaves me in command of the company. Before this I have spoken of Mike Foster's unparalleled bravery, and in all the late battles he has kept up his reputation for valor. Everyone who sees him during a battle is attracted by his fearlessness. If he were an officer, he would be distinguished. He fights because he enjoys the excitement. If he lives through the war, I imagine the life of an ordinary citizen will seem too tame for him. But not so with me. I long to get back to my dear home and to get to work again on the farm and in the mill. Not to be known, though, before an honorable peace is agreed upon.

It is now Nov. 14th, and I am detailed to take charge of a wagon train, but I find this kind of army duty so uncongenial to my taste that after I hold my position in that capacity one day, I get so homesick to get back to the command I just leave and arrive in camp by night. I find no difficulty in getting a substitute to take my place in the wagon train. We are now having quite a comfortable time, nothing sensational occurring. March a little, drill some, and stay in camp a greater portion of the time. I write home nearly every day and get many letters from the family. This gives me a greater satisfaction than I can express.

chapter twenty-two

FREDERICKSBURG

It is now the first of December and we are ordered to Fredericksburg. General Burnside is making demonstrations towards crossing the Rappahannock. On this march we pass a cotton field and although the crop has been partly picked, it is a great curiosity to many of us. On the night of the eleventh we camp twelve miles from Fredericksburg, and we have orders to cook three days' rations. Next morning at the first dawn of day, the Federal artillery opens vigorously, from Stafford Heights, while ours reply rather feebly. We are at once ordered to the front and we get near Fredericksburg by noon. The enemy by this time is occupying the town. The artillery fire keeps up until Burnside passes his army over the river. Now night comes on, and we sleep on our arms out of sight of the enemy. We are allowed to have some fire since the weather is cold and dry snow is falling.

Next morning, the 13th of December, both armies seem ready for the conflict. Jackson's corps is rapidly formed in lines of battle, the Stonewall Brigade being in the second line. Just before the battle opens in earnest, General Jackson rides along our lines. He has on a handsome new suit of grey cloth, presented to him by General Stuart. He makes such a fine appearance that at first we do not recognize him, but in a few minutes we hear the exclamation, "Why, that is old Jack!" The exclamations pass all along the lines. He is in company with Generals Lee, Stuart, and Longstreet, all of whom are reviewing, through their field glasses, the approach of the Federal army. It is reported that just then Longstreet said to Jackson, "General, do not all these multitudes frighten you?" It is said his reply was, "You shall see very soon if I do not frighten them."

The tremendous army keeps steadily advancing in lines of battle. It is the largest that ever invaded Virginia, numbering one hundred and twenty thousand and making the grandest military display I ever saw or expect to see. How could anything of this same character exceed this gorgeous exhibition of military perfection! The elegant and showy outfit of this huge Federal army. How superlatively grand and dreadful it looks to us Confederates who are so poorly clad and equipped and so inferior in numbers. There is one thing we certainly are proud of, though, and that is "Old Jack," who has such a splendid new suit of the somber grey with only enough gilt to mark his rank. He does look modest compared to the showy blue, glittering with tinsel in the bright morning sun, that adorns the Federal dress from a corporal up to the Commander-in-Chief. Even the privates look like an immense array of cadets from some great military school out on parade. Do not imagine, however, that we "rebel boys" feel the least bit ashamed, though some of us may be a little scared. But there is no indication of those tremors.

The fighting becomes general with the advantage of position entirely on our side, though at one point the enemy breaks our first line, commanded by General Gregg. As he pushed forward to reinstate his line, he was mortally wounded. Here was a great confusion. General Jackson orders up the second line. We push forward at a double-quick with the rebel yell and we soon drive the invaders from the woods. We pursue them with heavy loss across the railroad and into the fields beyond. This is an easy task compared to some things we have been through, notwithstanding the vast odds against which we have to contend. Their reserves are continually pouring in and the powerful artillery from Stafford Heights keeps up its terrible roar, sending out a fearful storm of shot and shell. This mostly goes over us.

It seems as though Burnside's great superiority of numbers does not do him any good, for he does not use his men to advantage. The situation looks to us as though he is just driving his magnificent army, dazzling in its grandness, into a slaughter pen for us to destroy. We feel like it is only child's play for us to do it, owing to our great advantage in position, for we are sheltered in a measure by a woodland. We withstand their charge and we drive them back with great loss to them. Although Jackson's corps has suffered severe loss, I believe we might have been equally successful with but half of our men engaged, inferior as our force in numbers is to the enemy's.

To show you how thick the iron hail fell around us I will mention that I noticed a small twig only eighteen inches long, that had been struck by nine balls. The firing soon ceases, except from the skirmishers, and night comes on. Thus ends the Battle of Fredericksburg. The enemy's loss is thirteen thousand and ours is four thousand two hundred. Jackson's Corps lost nearly three-fourths of this number. It is the price we paid for the post of honor.

The Federal army is in a fearfully critical condition. A report has just reached us that General Jackson has suggested to Generals Lee, Longstreet and Stuart that the Confederates, under cover of darkness, charge the enemy at once in their disorganized condition. General Jackson's plan is said to be that we remove our pants, in order to be easily distinguished from the Federals, but the report goes on further that the other Generals oppose such a measure. It may be that Jackson never made such a suggestion and that it never originated at headquarters at all. But if an idea of that nature has entered Jackson's mind, all he has to do is to shape it into an order and his men will obey, however desperate and cruel it may appear. We think it can be done with small loss to the Confederates but utter destruction to the enemy. However, this report is not likely to be anything real, for by this time, "Old Jack" would have been about through with his job. The soldiers think it quite possible that he did suggest something of the kind for it is very much like him. He believes in following up great victories and in making the most of them by inflicting irreparable loss upon the enemy. While there has been fearful destruction in the grand Federal army so thoroughly equipped, there are tremendous numbers still left and plenty of resources to bring up. If we had charged it might have been very confusing and have brought great loss to us. The fight may open again in the morning.

We watch for awhile, but about midnight Col. Shiver, who started out in the beginning of the war as Captain of the Shiver Grays of Wheeling, proposed to me that we lie down and sleep. So he and I bunk together in the railroad ditch. He being a large man gets more than his share of the blankets, and I wake up a little before day nearly frozen.

The morning shows the Federalists still drawn up in lines of battle, but the day wears away without any demonstration except the skirmishing of the sharpshooters and the fire from their artillery. The enemy seems to be strengthening their position. During the night of the 14th we hold the same lines. During Monday, the 15th, the enemy sends a flag of truce, asking permission to remove their wounded and bury their dead. Many have been lying on the frozen ground for two days. Permission is granted, hostilities cease, and officers and men from both armies mingle in friendly intercourse. The second day after the battle was ended we were very much in hopes the enemy would again attack on the morrow. But with the morning comes a sad surprise. We find that all the "live" portion of the Federal army has crossed over the Rappahannock. To our horror we find many dead men tied up to posts appearing like a picket force. Burnside, having ordered them to be placed to deceive us while he got his army over the river, left dead men to cover his retreat, showing that he knows what to do with dead men, if he didn't know how to handle live ones. The weather had favored them. There was a rain storm and a big wind from the South, which deadened the sound of their retreat during the night.

There seems to be no indication that there will be any more fighting now for awhile, and we hope the campaign has ended until spring. We are ordered to build winter quarters near Guinea Station, some ten miles from Fredericksburg, and in one week's time we are quite comfortable, with cabins large enough to accommodate from four to ten persons. Captains Frazier and

Snyder, Lieutenant Whittaker, and myself have a cabin together and we are as snug and cozy as we could wish. We have a good chimney to our room, built of wood and mortar. Our bunks are raised from the ground with pine brush laid on them, bed clothes on top of that and then plenty of blankets to cover with. Comparing our present comfort with what our condition has often been since we joined the army, we feel like it is indeed the zenith of comfort. Truly we estimate nearly everything by comparison. Soldiering is a fine chance to find out how little man really needs to keep life going and even to give some comfort. Now, as much as we appreciate our comfort, there is one thing we appreciate even more, and that is the opportunity to keep clean our persons, clothes, beds and cabins. No one but a good solider can understand the amount of discomfort we have had to endure from not having a chance to "clean up."

As the winter progresses, we have regular drill once a day. We also have regular religious services both Sabbath mornings and nights and Wednesday nights. We have three chaplains to our Brigade, Mr. Vass of the 27th Regiment who is a Presbyterian, Mr. A.C. Hopkins, chaplain of the 2nd Regiment who is also a Presbyterian, and the 4th Regiment has a Baptist minister as chaplain. I forget his name. They are all faithful, earnest, Christian workers. Each chaplain has particular charge over his own regiment, somewhat like a pastor has over a congregation. Mr. Vass comes in our cabin very frequently and talks to us on religious subjects and the welfare of our souls, often praying with us. I feel a deep attachment for him. He has been chaplain of our regiment for more than two months. I should have mentioned him before this. He preaches the Word publicly and from cabin to cabin as he has opportunity. He is a faithful shepherd and a brave "soldier of the cross," never shirking duty no matter where or when it calls. We have a good church built of round logs and put up by we soldiers as we were detailed to work each day, each as our turn came. We were very little over a week building it for there was a big force working on it every day. When an army turns out to do a job it is soon finished. There is one great drawback to it. There is no way to heat it. It seems to me that with so many willing workers we might have built a rough chimney that would have been safe. It would have added greatly to our comfort. We have plenty of good provisions and a colored man named Jim to cook for us. All of us are in good health and very happy.

It is now near the middle of February and as I stand in my cabin door I see an old gentleman with a long gray beard come walking. On looking closely I see it is a friend of my parents, Mr. C.L. Peyton, father of my friend Thomas Peyton. He is nearby and I call to him that his father is coming and we both walk rapidly to meet him. How good a civilian does look! The greeting between father and son is an affectionate one and makes me think of another dear old man of the Greenbrier Valley whom I hope to see soon. The soldiers are being furloughed. I have made my application for one and am impatiently waiting my turn. Mr. Peyton stays with us several days and we all, officers and men, vie with each other in trying to make him comfortable and in providing something nice for him to eat. He is such a kind, genial, Christian gentleman. We have great respect for his long gray beard. (We seldom see gray hairs in the army.) Altogether it is a great treat to hear him talk and we gather around him in crowds. He is such an enthusiastic Southerner as well as such a humble Christian. He gives us good advice and further encourages us by his hearty sympathy. Tom does not get much private intercourse with his father. I feel sometimes as if we other boys are real selfish to intrude on his time so much. Mr. Peyton has just left and we feel lost, but I am expecting every day to get my furlough.

chapter twenty-three

SECOND FURLOUGH

It is now the 20th of February, 1863, and I start on my second furlough to again visit by dear home. I have some comrades with me who also have furloughs. We walk as far as Guinea Station where we take the train. We have to travel the Virginia and Tennessee railroad as the Virginia Central is not safe for we soldier boys. The Federal troops often make demonstrations in that direction. We go to Bonsack's Depot. From there we walk about fifty miles. We are much hindered in our journey by high waters, especially Craig's and Potts' Creeks. We come on together to Monroe County, the other boys taking their routes homeward and I going on towards Lewisburg. An old acquaintance in Monroe loaned me a mule which I ride home. It is nearly dark when I get in sight of home. I stop a few minutes at my sister's house and then hurry on to see my dear parents who are taken greatly by surprise. I had written that I hoped soon to get a furlough but, of course, I could not specify the time, not knowing when my furlough would come.

As soon as the family greeting is over, I make a request that somewhat shocks the sensibilities of the whole family, namely, that a tub of warm water, towels and soap, and an entire change of clothing for me be taken to an outhouse in the backyard, so that I can get rid of the company I brought with me before I take my seat with the family around the fireside. I tell them they may not find the "gray backs" very desirable. It does not take me long to get through my ablutions and I come back to the house dressed in an entirely different outfit, even to my shoes. I leave my army clothes in the yard. I feel once more like a clean, respectable citizen. As I come in I pass through the kitchen and am there welcomed by the servants, all of whom are still here except John, who has gone to the Yankees. He was a large, fine-looking, very dark, colored man, a brother to Caesar. The latter seems to be as faithful as ever, as well as his two young brothers, his mother, Maria, and sister, Mary. All seem contented and happy. My father and brother think John was enticed away by another Negro belonging to a neighbor, but I imagine his going is only the beginning of what is to follow.

I find that the war cloud has been hanging dark and threatening over my home on the dear old Greenbrier. On my first visit home it seemed to a Stonewall veteran very peaceful indeed, but now I find the impress of this cruel war here as well as in the more eastern portion of Virginia. The Federals have a considerable force at Meadow Bluff, a point twelve miles west of Lewisburg. Their cavalry often dash in unexpectedly to Lewisburg and vicinity, soldiers often coming as far east as the Greenbrier River. The Confederates claim to hold the country on the south and east banks, so my father's house is just on the line, making the situation just about like my brother Tom describes it, "alternating between bands of robbers and gangs of beggars." The Federal scouts, who are watching the Confederates, and claim the country west of the Greenbrier, come foraging through the neighborhood, taking all they can find for man or beast to eat, thus leaving the people destitute. The most natural thing for the wives and children of southern men who are in the army is to come to "Edgar's Mill" for bread-stuff. And frequently they find but little left, only what careful vigilance on the part of my brother, assisted by Mr. Toothman and our colored men, who put all eatables for man or beast all out of sight as nearly as possible, before the robbers can get them, as they are generally expected to visit the mill first. Nevertheless, they are not infrequently hurried off by little reminders from the guns of the Confederates, pickets and bushwhackers that come whigging from across the river, thus causing the Federals to fail in making as thorough a search as they wish, and leaving more for the women and children. But what remains is always divided out among the helpless applicants, as everything that will make the "staff of life" is held in common at the mill just after these raids occur.

While we listened to all this news we all sat around the supper table, but our hearts are too full of gratitude for our reunion, without a number of the family being missing, for the craving of our stomachs to be thought much about. Time to retire for the night comes and all of us are under the dear old home roof again. How can we be thankful enough while so many others have not been so mercifully dealt with? I still declined sleeping in a sure enough bed, but am willing to try sleeping on a lounge in the sitting room instead of the floor, as I have been promoted to a bunk in a comfortable cabin for the past two months. When morning comes I am happier than I have been since my last furlough, for we have not yet commenced to count the days until I must leave again. My mother's health is about as good as it was when I was home before, but it is evident that my father is rapidly failing in strength. How sad the thought of leaving him again is to me!

I have now been at home more than a week and am enjoying walking about the farm with my father and brother and any friend who comes to see me. I occasionally go back to the house to talk with my mother and sisters, sometimes taking my meals with my oldest sister, Mrs. Creigh. She and her husband, when he's at home, come in and eat with us, the homes not being more than 200 yards apart. Time is rapidly passing and we have come to the 7th of March. My furlough more than half gone, I do not visit any because I have no desire to do so, for one thing, and then it is nothing unusual for raiding parties of the enemy to dash in and out again. And if they should see a Confederate soldier, it seems not likely they would pass him by unmolested, so the most prudent thing for me to do is to stay indoors. I have been hearing so much of the details concerning the Battle of Lewisburg, that I have concluded to write some of the facts down in this reminiscence, as I would like to preserve that part of its history which immediately concerns our family.

chapter twenty-four

A DIGRESSION: THE BATTLE OF LEWISBURG

This battle occurred the 23rd of May, 1862, and, of course, does not belong to my war experience, but as it happened so near my home, I have been greatly interested in it ever since I read of it in the newspapers and the home letters. But now that I am at home and we can talk it all over, I hear the most interesting facts from the lips of my father and brother, who were eye witnesses of the battle. I think it will make this reminiscence more interesting to the Edgar family. Anyhow, I have some of the facts connected with it, that most intimately concerns the family, written down here, though some might consider it out of place.

On the evening before the battle occurred, our family had been informed by the Confederate Scouts that it would take place at early dawn on the next morning. So my father and brother, in company with three of our neighbors, Mrs. William Vogelsong, Randolph Morgan, and David L. Creigh, concluded they would go to the suburbs of Lewisburg and witness a battle. As they passed Dr. Creigh's, two miles south of Lewisburg, Mr. James Fisk, a gentleman from Washington City, who is boarding there with his family, joined them and they all went as near as Wagner's Hill, as they thought safe – a highpoint, where the Confederate artillery was stationed. The enemy being encamped on the western hill, had no artillery worth speaking of and were taken entirely by surprise, when our artillery opened on them, thus giving the advantage of making the attack as well as of position. Gen. Heath was commander of the Confederate force, and from all accounts, very incompetent to fill his position. The firing only lasted 20 minutes, artillery and small arms included, ending in utter defeat and route to the Confederate Gen. Heath, making the great mistake of having his artillery force leave their fine position and run down into the middle of the town that was a regular hollow. The enemy, taking advantage of this mistake, divided their force and was about to surround the township and, of course, there was nothing else left to do but for the Confederates to run as quickly as possible. So they did just what the Yankees expected in the song they composed about the battle.

"They scampered down the ridge;
Burnt the river bridge;
And traveled to the happy land of Canaan."

It is said that some of the artillerists sent Gen. Heath word after the fight that they hoped he would provide bayonets for their guns before they were ordered into another battle. Although the little encounter lasted such a short time it was a bloody one, the Confederates having 23 killed on the field and as many more mortally wounded, some of them dying within 24 hours after the battle and still more seriously wounded. It is said the Federals lost as many as we did. But they took both their dead and wounded so far back in the direction of Meadow Bluff that no one about here saw any of them. Some of our neighbors were killed and wounded in the fight. Mr. Joseph Rourke, who was my father's miller when I can first remember, had a son, George Washington, mortally wounded. He died the next day after the battle.

Major Edgar, a cousin of ours (his father and mine were brothers), was shot through the body near one of his lungs and was thought to be mortally wounded. The report reached my father's house that he was killed on the field. My sister, Mrs.

A Digression: The Battle of Lewisburg

Creigh, started at once for Lewisburg walking accompanied by Mrs. Robinson, a neighbor whose husband was supposed to have been in the battle. Their reason for walking to Lewisburg was that to have attempted any other mode of locomotion on that day, would have meant being sent out in the road on foot, and horse and carriage and driver appropriated to United States service. However they reached the town safely, though very tired. My sister found to her great joy that Major Edgar was still living, though dangerously wounded, and that there was considerable hope of his recovery. They were also told that General Crook, the Federal commander, had just issued an order that all citizens who wished either to enter or to leave this town, must do so immediately or not at all that day and possibly not the next. My sister and Mrs. Robinson went to his headquarters and requested him to give them a pass that would admit them of their remaining half an hour. They pleaded that each of them had friends engaged in the battle whom they were very anxious about and begged for a few minutes indulgence. General Crook answered "No" in a gruff voice. Looking at his watch he said, "The time is already passed and you may not have a pass at all. You will have to wait for future developments." The General had been wounded in the head and did not feel very amiable towards the "Rebs," although he had wished them well. The two women did not give up hope of getting out of town that day. The first thing to do was to find out more about Major Edgar and Mr. Robinson. My sister was told by her friends that Major Edgar was taken to the house of Mr. John Withrow, a first cousin of his and ours. He was being attended by Dr. Anderson and two Federal surgeons. As he was at the house of Cousin John he was having the tenderest care so there was no necessity for my sister to remain. More especially no one was permitted to see him but his nurses and physicians. Then Cousin James Withrow and his family, residents of Lewisburg, will give all necessary assistance. Mrs. Robinson soon found out that her husband had not been in the fight. The wisest thing for them to do was to resort to some sort of stratagem to evade Yankee vigilance and, thereby, get out of town. There was work for them to do where they were helping care for the wounded. Many of the public buildings and some private dwellings had been converted into hospitals and much work was to be done for the suffering. The citizens of Lewisburg were prompt to offer their assistance, which they could do and yet not cut themselves off from their homes, as would my sister and Mrs. Robinson. They felt that their duty was at home under the circumstances. They walked about a square from General Crook's headquarters, where they discovered one of our neighbors, Mrs. Jesse J. Livesay, on horseback. (She afterwards told my sister that she felt that if the Yankees did covet old "Gray Dick" enough to set her off in the road, she would not be much poorer as he was twenty-one years old and could claim nothing in the way of beauty to tempt them, as he had got to be a flea-bitten gray.) Mrs. Livesay was followed by at least a dozen women and boys on foot. My sister and Mrs. Robinson hurried on and joined the crowd. They told Mrs. Livesay that they were in a trap, General Crook refusing to give them a pass. "Follow me," she said, "and I will take you through." "But, Mrs. Livesay, I'm afraid your pass is only sufficient for you and your followers here," replied my sister. In an undertone, Mrs. Livesay insisted, "come on, fall into the crowd." They meekly obeyed with fluttering hearts. Mrs. Livesay handed her pass to one of the picket guard, who read it and looked closely at it. (Mrs. Livesay thought most of them were foreigners and could not read or speak English). The guard frowned, looked over the frightened crowd of women and boys and handed the pass to one of his comrades. This man looked more like he read it. He handed it back to Mrs. Livesay and said in a gruff voice, "Pass on." They passed on, without delay, between cavalrymen, two on either side of the road, sitting on their restive horses champing their bits, while the war accoutrements clanked around them. They came to the next picket force, just out of the sight of the first, and on to still a third, all passing them in about the same surly manner. At the last post the officer in command kept the pass and tore it up. Mrs. Livesay asked him if they were clear from there on. He nodded his head and motioned her on. The road that led to Edgar's Ford seemed to be looked upon by the Federal Army, when they were trying to hold Lewisburg, with more apprehension than any other which led out of town. To go or come between my father's house and Lewisburg, when the Federals were there, meant to

A Digression: The Battle of Lewisburg

run a gauntlet of Yankee pickets for at least a mile outside the town. This was somewhat trying to the nerves of civilians and they avoided it whenever possible. After that, this group had no trouble. When my sister got home, she found that one or two companies of Federals had been down as far as my father's house and her's. They had searched for live, dead, or wounded Rebel soldiers, firearms, and last, but not least, something to eat, which they felt no hesitancy in helping themselves, until the house was destitute of cooked provision. They then ordered biscuits to be baked, but not feeling safe five miles from their headquarters, they ate them half-baked, and left without doing any damage to property. Going on to my sister's and finding no one at home (the servants had become frightened and run to my father's), they tried the doors, but not being able to get in, they raised the dining room window. They saw the breakfast table within reach, with some of the breakfast dishes left on it because of the great excitement when the firing in Lewisburg was heard. They helped themselves to five silver spoons and half a dozen knives and forks. So much for the house being left alone at such a time.

Major Edgar continued to improve. The Federals moved back as far as Meadow Bluff, but still claimed to hold the town by sending a squad of cavalry to dash in every day and remain an hour or so. My father's family managed to evade them and drove in every few days to see Major Edgar. In a few weeks he was able to sit up and walk through his room. By that time, the Federals began showing signs of falling back from Meadow Bluff even. His friends became anxious for fear they would take him before he was quite strong and expose him to prison fare, which might prove fatal. So, that part of the Confederate Army which was stationed five or six miles southwest of Greenbrier River sent a squad of cavalry, which carried him inside the Confederate line. This was very much a surprise to him as well as to the Lewisburg relatives and my father's family, for it seemed to be a question in their minds whether it was the proper thing to do or not. But it was military power and neither citizens or Major Edgar could control the case. The first intimation my father's family had of this, was when the cavalry stopped at the gate and demanded "a suitable conveyance to go to Lewisburg and take Major Edgar inside the Confederate lines." Mr. Creigh hurried and got his double buggy which could be drawn out to a greater length than my father's carriage. He then went with them to Lewisburg. It was about an hour after dark that they got Major Edgar, all unexpected to himself and to the Withrow's, and against their will. It was a risk for him over rough roads at night, but it was done under military orders and could not be objected to by citizens or Major Edgar himself. He was taken to the house of a friend, with a considerable Confederate force between him and the Federals, and good care was taken of him until he got well. His long, rough nocturnal ride did him no harm. At the end of two or three months he was duly exchanged and later on fought in a successful little battle three miles north of Lewisburg, called the "Battle of Tuckwiller's Mill." No Confederates were engaged in the fight aside from his battalion, while the Federals had a whole regiment marching on Lewisburg. He turned them back, not allowing them to get into town at all at that time, without any loss on his side. I believe if he had been in command at the Battle of Lewisburg there would have been a very different result. Still later, he and his battalion were engaged in the Battle of White Sulphur Springs. Colonel Patton was in command of the Confederate force, which was victorious there but could hold the ground only at intervals.

Now we have come to the tenth of March and in just two days I must again leave my dear home and can think of nothing else. My dear parents, especially my old father, are so feeble. Will a merciful God permit me to come back again and find all here?

chapter twenty-five

Battle of Chancellorsville and Jackson's Death

The morning of the twelfth of March, 1863, has come and I must bid goodbye to my dear old home and start back to camp. No stages are running now. Tom, my brother, takes me on horseback to Bonsack's Depot, a trip of two days. There I bid him goodbye with a sad heart. From there I went by rail to Guinea Station. I found everything just as I had left it. I went into the same cabin and felt that I could make myself quite comfortable if it were not that I had just left my own dear home. I was so homesick for that spot that I could take no pleasure in anything for awhile.

We stayed in camp until April the twenty-ninth, with nothing unusual taking place. We had drill and church service just as we usually did. I received a letter from home telling me of the birth of a little nephew, my sister's son, whom they have named for me – Alfred Edgar.

The Federals were crossing the Rappahannock and everybody in camp was astir. We had orders to cook several days' rations and be ready to march at a moment's warning. The weather was getting quite warm and we felt reluctant to leave

Battle of Chancellorsville and Jackson's Death

our old camp. We were marched and counter-marched around considerably. The Federals frequently made feints to cross the river at points. By the first day of May they had occupied the high ground around Chancellorsville and had a very fine position. A portion of Longstreet's corps was still absent. Our army, all told, numbered only between thirty and forth thousand. The Federal Army was said to number 80,000. We were within a few miles of the Federals. The whole country around us is known as the "wilderness" and was covered with a scrubby, almost impassable brush. I never saw such dense brush before.

The whole of the first day of May was used by our Generals, as we supposed, to contrive some sort of strategy against "fighting Joe Hooker," the commander of the Federal forces. Our force was too small to engage his great army in front fight. We bivouacked that night and our rations were cooked and brought to us.

In the morning there was a report in camp that Generals Lee, Jackson, and Stuart sat up all night trying to devise some plan to draw Hooker out of his strong position. Jackson proposed to be allowed to take his corps to the rear of Hooker's Army, leaving Lee with two divisions of Longstreet's corps.

At nine o'clock Jackson's corps was ordered to march. At that time we did not know where. We had not gone far when we observed a balloon high up in the air sent up by the enemy. It was fired on at frequent interval by our artillery but without effect. We had orders to move briskly and be as quiet as possible so that the enemy might not know our whereabouts. But they discovered our movements from the balloon and reported that the Rebel army was retreating toward Richmond. Our march continued until we reached the Chancellorsville turnpike, fifteen miles from where we started.

Here we found a large body of Stuart's cavalry, which reported that the Federals were totally ignorant of our close proximity and intention and that they are preparing to bivouac. We were stopped for an hour so that the rear division might close up. We were formed in line of battle and ordered to leave all our baggage except our ordinance.

At three p.m. Jackson sent Lee word that he was now ready to make the attack. Here we were in the most dense part of the wilderness on the right side of the turnpike. Rode's division was in front and Colston's division, to which I belonged, following close after, then Hill's division in marching order on the turnpike. We now had orders to go forward, but we had to move cautiously as our guns were loaded and the thick brush might catch the triggers and set them off. It was utterly impossible for our lines to be kept in order because of the extreme density of the brush. We struggled on in this toilsome way for about half a mile, when Rode's division became engaged with the enemy. The "Rebel Yell" was heard in such frightfully shrill notes that the enemy was at once repulsed and fell back pell mell. By this time our division became merged with Rode's and the greatest confusion followed. Orders were sent to us by General Jackson to press forward. It was now near night and we were hungry and worn out and still the awful confusion increased because of the brush. But still the orders were to press forward. We soon ran upon the enemy's breastworks and stockade combined. It was strongly manned.

Our situation was becoming very critical by reason of our proximity to this powerful Federal force and being cut off from a large portion of our army, small as it is. To add to our peril we were getting so mixed up none of us knew where we belonged in the confusion and darkness. Jackson quickly took in the situation. He kept sending orders by subordinate officers. "Get into line." "Get into line." "Men, do get into line." To obey that order promptly seemed to us an impossibility because of the fast approaching darkness and the cruel brush which threatened to set off our guns and tear out our eyes. Thousands of voices were calling out,

"Where is Colston's division?"

"Where is Rode's division?"

"Where is Hill's division?"

And as many voices were answering,

"Here is Colston's."

"Here is Rode's."

"Here is Hill's."

What good voices amid all this confusion!

At this time we discovered that the enemy had left the breastworks. Quiet and order were restored to a certain extent.

But we could not tell what division was in front, most probably Hill's. We were all suffering from hunger and fatigue. Yet we were amused when a poor hungry-looking greenhorn came along. With haggard visage and in the most pitiful tones he asked if we had seen anything of the third Alabama pot wagon, meaning the wagon that contained their cooking utensils. After that we called our provision wagons the "pot" wagons.

We found plenty of cooked food of good quality and coffee prepared for us by men detailed for that purpose. We supplied ourselves with overcoats and blankets left by the enemy. We scattered through the brush and ate and rested.

Then came the news to officers of the rank of major upward that General Jackson was dangerously wounded. The men and lower officers were not to know. I was only a first lieutenant and was not informed. But I noticed the extreme excitement and distress indicated in our adjutant's manner and asked him what dreadful thing had happened. He whispered the appalling news to me, but cautioned me not to let anyone know. I felt like the very earth was sinking under me but tried not to show any sign of my feelings in my manner. But in a few moments the news seemed to have gone through rank and file and we heard exclamations of sorrow. We tried to comfort ourselves with the hope that the report might be much exaggerated and that our beloved, gallant and God-fearing commander might soon be well and able to lead us into battle. We felt that he was guided directly from the mouth of Jehovah as was Joshua when he led the Israelites to battle. This we felt almost to the verge of idolatry. I have always thought of Stonewall Jackson's pure character as he led us on in the strength of the Lord as similar to Joshua's. His extreme valor and coolness coupled with a humble Christian faith and endurance inspired us with a feeling of adoration that was a species of idolatry. I believe the same feeling pervaded most of the Stonewall brigade.

Now our empty stomachs and tired limbs claimed our rightful attention and we ate our supper and tried to sleep knowing that the morning would bring more danger and hardships that we would be utterly unfit for without a few hours sleep. We did get three or four hours of sleep which greatly refreshed us.

As day dawned we awakened and heard the circumstances concerning Jackson's being wounded. It seemed that he and his staff had ridden some distance in front of our line of battle as he was anxious to know more of the enemy's position. Jackson became so very anxious about the situation of our army that he forgot entirely his own and his staff's safety. It was just after Rode's division became engaged with the enemy and drove them back in such disorder. At the same time our division was merged with Rode's and great confusion followed. Just then, seeing the peril of the Confederate army, Jackson entirely lost sight of the distance that he was going, so that he was probably 100 yards or more in the direction of the enemy's line. The Confederates mistook him and his staff for a Federal cavalry advancing and fired a volley into their midst. The standing orders were that those in the front line must fire on anyone approaching, without hitting them. Thus, the disastrous wounding of our beloved General, the killing of the courageous Captain Boswell, one of the staff, and the wounding of others of his escort done by shots fired from the Confederate guns. How dark and mysterious is Providence.

On the third of May General Jeb Stuart was put in command of Jackson's corps at his (Jackson's) request. The artillery on both sides had, by nine o'clock, commenced a furious fire with our side getting the worst of the duel. The Federal army had the better position. The first order we received that day was "Charge and remember Jackson!"

The report was current that the 2nd Virginia Brigade refused to respond, but I do not know how true that was. I do know that as we passed over what had been the Federal breastworks that Brigade was lying down in our way and one great big man told me to set my foot on his shoulder and pass over, which I did. They may have been ordered to lie down.

We drove the enemy from their position, but they had a second line of battle, which stopped our ordinance. We met the heaviest, bloodiest infantry fire I had been exposed to. General Stuart was charged with reckless daring and exposing his men to unnecessary danger. I cannot see the case in that light. Five men belonging to my company were killed within fifteen minutes. Among them was George Harper, one of the best and most courageous soldiers who ever shouldered a gun. He was from Greenbrier and an acquaintance of mine. He was shot in the mouth. He walked to a tree, stood his gun against it, stepped up to me, took me by the shoulder, attempted to say something and feel dead at my feet.

Before we made this charge a few men from the regiment were detailed with orders to shoot any man who attempted to go to the rear or shirk duty. After half an hour's firing we were reinforced by a brigade coming up and drove the enemy some distance. It is true that the Stonewall Brigade stood alone thirty-five minutes before two enemy lines of battle. Afterward we drove the enemy to the next hill top where they made another stand. We found many dead men on the ground and some riderless horses. One we captured but found to be worthless because of a foot wound.

The enemy made a stand at the Chancellor house and we charged them, raising the "Rebel Yell" vigorously. We found the Chancellor house set fire by our shells and many of the wounded Federals burning to death. This house was General Hookers' headquarters. We moved these men out of danger. This was the last we saw of the Yankees at this time, for they were completely routed and disappeared in the dense thickets. We went three or four miles to the right and encamped for the night.

In the morning we found that the Federals had all crossed over the Rappahannock. That same day we were moved to a camping ground six or eight miles from Guinea Station. We heard from Jackson every day, but there was not much encouragement. We feared that he was gradually growing worse. We were moved about five miles in the direction of Guinea Station and remained there a week. Each day we heard bad news from General Jackson and at last comes the worst of all, that he is dead! We felt that all was lost. Deeply we mourned our greatly honored and much beloved commander and trembled for the Confederacy, feeling assured that a mystic power of guidance obtained at a throne of grace by the constant and fervent prayers for Jackson has gone from our confederacy. The loss is irreparable. Most especially do we who belonged to the Stonewall Brigade feel the crushing loss, as though our most reliable motive power had gone, and with it our energy and confidence of success. I could just then realize that the Stonewall Brigade looked upon Jackson with a degree of worship that was too much akin to worship and an all-wise God had to remove him. We actually felt that it was impossible to fail when he was leading us. One thing we knew, that God can make no mistake, however dark and mysterious His providence may seem to mortals. Our beloved Jackson's work on earth was done or he would not have been taken from us and although in the prime of his life and at the zenith of earthly aggrandizement as a noble military genius and a humble exemplary Christian gentleman. Viewing it from a human standpoint he had so much to live for and so much work still to do. Yet the summons came. "Behold the bridegroom cometh, go ye out to meet him." He found him with his lamp trimmed and brightly burning, able to go with joy and not with sorrow.

An order came for seventy-five men from the Stonewall Brigade to be detailed to escort his body to Richmond. Two officers, a captain and a lieutenant, were to be of the detail. I was honored by being chosen for the latter officer. New clothing had just been issued and I had the nicest suit of uniform that I had worn. All of the boys were nicely dressed up. Those who were unfortunate not to have suitable clothing of their own, borrowed from friends. So we were a quite fine looking company as we started on our mournful mission. We hurried off and got dressed as soon as possible after the order came. When we arrived at Guinea station, we were greatly disappointed to find that the train had been gone an hour or more. We slowly retraced our steps to camp, finding it hard to reconcile the bitter disappointment.

I must say just here, as I have been informed, that General Jackson had learned a short time before he was wounded that there was a Federal corps threatening his flank. When crossing at one of the fords on the Rappahannock, he sent one of his regiments, to get as near the enemy as possible without endangering themselves. They fired three vollies and then returned to their places. It had the effect he intended as in the next days fight the Federal general did not appear on the battle field. This was about the last order Jackson gave before he was wounded and it has proved to be a stratagem of great value to the Confederates, in as much as it kept off a large Federal force, that they otherwise would have been obliged to have encountered.

We remained two weeks longer in the camp and were then ordered to the Valley. General Ewell took command of the Second Corps. We soon noticed that our march was not so hurried as when Jackson commanded. We made only about twelve or fifteen miles in a day's march. It seems slow moving to us of Jackson's Corps, especially his old brigade.

chapter twenty-six

GETTYSBURG

General Lee's objective now is to capture the Federal force that occupied Winchester. Winchester was our objective point. As our column marched through Front Royal, all the citizens came out to cheer us. They were overjoyed to see us once more.

We crossed the Shenandoah and came to Cedarville where we rested for the night. In the morning we took the road to the Valley Pike. On the thirteenth our column divided, our division keeping the Front Royal road, while Early's division took another road. We had had some hard fighting since we left the dear old valley the past autumn.

Ten miles from the town of Winchester we made a line of battle and began to skirmish on the morning of the fourteenth. Our division moved forward, the Stonewall Brigade leading and renewed the skirmishing. In the afternoon we heard the sound of Early's guns. Just before night we received orders to move by right flank to the Martinsburg turnpike at a point beyond Winchester. The other brigades started at once across the country. But the Stonewall Brigade being nearest the enemy are ordered to advance skirmishers to conceal the movement from the men and then to follow the other brigade. There was some delay in the receipt of the order and we did not take the road by which the other brigade marched until midnight. We grow very tired but are urged to press forward. When we reach the Valley Pike by morning we find the enemy retreating, evacuating Winchester. The Yankees are running as fast as they can. We too are running as fast as we can and yelling our best. Mike Foster in front. We capture more than two thousand prisoners with arms and equipment and a great many horses. We soon hear that Gen. Early has captured more in the town with 25 pieces of artillery, ammunition, and three hundred loaded wagons. But the greatest part of Milroy's command evacuated the town in the early part of the night and so got away from us and is retreating as fast as possible towards the Potomac. Thus ends the Second Battle of Winchester. It looks like a farce to call it a battle. It is certainly a bloodless victory, but we have had some very bloody ones, so this is a desirable change, if it is somewhat tame. We may have more bloody ones in the future and I greatly fear bloody failures also. "The end is not yet."

It is now the 15th of June, 1863. The health of the army has greatly improved since coming back to the beloved Valley. During the winter while we were in camp so long, many of us took scurvy and were not in good health, but now since we can get plenty of vegetables to eat and kind words of welcome to cheer us up, our health is about perfect. Our army has greatly improved in number and efficiency. We have the spoils of great battlefields. Artillery, cavalry, and infantry are so much better equipped from our vast captured supplies. It is said that the army now numbers 73,000 men. The spirit of the army is fine and we are eager for action. But still we of Jackson's Corps still miss our beloved leader.

We start today on our second invading expedition. It is rumored that the army will invade Pennsylvania. Our marching is different from what it was when Stonewall Jackson was leading us. We now march quietly along, no hurried order. We of his old corps cannot but note the difference and whilst we are eager for more victories, we do not feel that we can do the efficient work we were to do under him. It is now the

18th of June and our corps crosses the Potomac with the bands playing "Maryland, My Maryland." We march more rapidly now through Maryland into Pennsylvania. We find the richest and most plentiful country that we have ever been in since the war began. It is hard to realize that the Valley of Virginia once looked this way, before it was devastated by war. We have the most rigid order not to molest or disturb private property. Our cavalry is many miles ahead of us, having started some days in advance of us. We scarcely ever see any kind of stock, especially are all the horses run off out of our way. Another thing draws our attention and amuses us very much. The farm wagons have but three wheels, the fourth one being invariably out of sight. But the farmers might just as well leave the fourth one on, the wagons being what is called broad tread and are useless and undesirable to us.

When we reach Chambersburg we stop one day to rest. I embrace the opportunity to walk through the town. All of the citizens are very hostile to us. No one has a civil word or look for us. In fact, they are very rude. This seems uncultured to us Southerners. In Dixie we treat everyone with a certain degree of politeness, even our slaves, but then we are chivalrous people. We have plenty of Confederate money and pay for everything we get, although the citizens are very much opposed to accepting our money, but we insist and they finally end by taking it. I bought the largest and best loaf of bread from a very cross woman for 50 cents. It was as large as a half bushel and perfect in quality. One could almost forgive her for her acidity when eating the bread.

We hear that Gen. Meade, who has superseded Hooker, is in the neighborhood of Frederick City and we "about face" in that direction. The Confederate army is in the best of health and finest spirits imaginable. The first day or two of our march is as quiet and comfortable as can be and brings us within 20 miles of Gettysburg. It is now the 30th of June, 1863, p.m. By noon the next day we are within eight or ten miles of Gettysburg and we hear cannon fire a long distance off and wonder what it means as we have no idea that we are so near the Federal army. The different corps of our army are coming from opposite points of the compass – Hill's, Longstreet's and Ewell's – Gettysburg being the common center. Hill's corps is hotly engaged by the time we are within five miles of them and we are hurried to his support. As we get there the enemy is repulsed and we only follow them within the bayonet. They retreat to the height overlooking Gettysburg with only a portion of their army up, while ours is nearly all on the ground. And right here is the place Gen. Lee made his mistake, that he did not push on and get position of those heights that evening.

It is now late in the afternoon and we bivouac for the night and are astir early in the morning of the 2nd, but only a portion of our army is actually engaged in the fighting. Our brigade is detached from the corps. Watching a heavy force of enemy cavalry that keep in sight of us all day, we heartily wished they would come up and allow us a chance at them. All the fighting that is done today is only preparatory for what is to come. Detached portions of both armies are fighting at different points with Gen. Longstreet's corps bearing the blunt. Night comes again and I am detached, under a field officer and 75 men under me for picket duty, and from what I can hear of the movements of the enemy, that they are making preparations for a desperate fight. I can hear them bring up their artillery and can tell from the noise and talking that their number must be very great. Two comrades and I myself crawled up to within hearing distance of the enemy's pickets and we heard them calling to their men to "fall in the Seventh Massachusetts." We want to report this but cannot find the supervisor officer. Longstreet's corps has had a hot engagement with the enemy during the day and met with a bloody repulse, not accomplishing what Gen. Lee intended him to do. Both armies sleep on their arms the night of the 2nd within gun shot of each other. At dawn of day on the 3rd, the great battle begins with furious desperation, the Confederates advancing to close quarters and the battle raging all along the line, the enemy keeping up the most destructive fire that has ever been during the war. Though Lee's lines being so long and his force so large that, of course, I cannot tell anything that is occurring except what is immediately around me. Any information that I am giving will necessarily seem tame and lean compared to what historians will certainly write hereafter. We veterans had thought we had been through much danger before and been exposed to powerful artillery and fearful infantry fires, and some frightful destruction of human life, but as we hear the terrific and deafening roar of their cannons and the men cut down as grain before the sickle, we conclude that all we have been through in the past is nothing but child's play compared to this and slides into utter insignificance.

Meade had 200 pieces of artillery belching forth their death dealing missiles, adding to a furious infantry fire. The dense smoke and stifling smell of powder makes us feel like the very great gate of Perdition must be thrown open and all the hellish horrors the imagination can depict thrown out to destroy us! At first the fire was not so destructive, but as the day advances and the enemy measures our distances, minnie balls and shells come lower and execute their works more fatally. Even the very air seems thick with the missiles of death, from the small arms as well as from the artillery. It seems impossible that any of us can live fifteen minutes longer exposed to so much fire. Yet I do not feel like I'm going to be killed now and just this moment a peaceful assurance falls on my soul as if coming from Jesus Himself, that it is perfectly safe, that His blood has been applied to it with all its cleansing power, and if my body should be shattered to pieces in a moment, it will only be to set my justified spirit free to be received in His outstretched arms, leaving my body, still united to Christ, although it might not be buried, to be raised up in glory at the last day.

It is now between 9 and 10 o'clock a.m., and our ammunition is getting very low. Our stock is being replenished by being carried to us in boxes put in the hands of the most fearless men, going to the rear and returning, placing themselves in more danger than we are who remain in the front all the time. Our wounded are being poorly cared for by this time, as the ambulance corps seem to be inadequate in the work they have to do. Although they wear red caps and their dress is otherwise conspicuous, I have not seen one of them for two hours and then he was running as fast as his legs could carry him with a wounded man on his back. I don't mean they are cowardly. Oh, no! They are chosen from our best and bravest men, but now I believe they have become entirely discouraged with the immensity of their work and I give up in despair as most of them may be wounded and killed. That they may be wounded or killed, the fact remains the same that their failure to appear adds greatly to the horrors of the situation. As the day still advances, the firing from the enemy gets heavier and the carnage and bloodshed more frightful. The wounded and dying are literally heaping up around us and their groans and cries for help and mercy rise above the roar of the battle. One poor fellow, an acquaintance of mine, has just died at my feet with his imploring eyes fixed on me. There are many, many others just close around me that I know are mortally wounded, some of them dying and some of them that might be saved with proper care. That poor fellow that bled to death might have been, but I can't leave my post of duty a moment. All I can do is raise the humble petition to heaven, "Lord Jesus, pardon their sins and receive their spirits." Still the battle rages with increased fury. How much longer, oh, how much longer, gracious and merciful Father in Heaven, must this appalling destruction of human life continue, until Thy all wise and mysterious purpose is accomplished?

It is now about 11 o'clock a.m., and Pickett makes his charge on the little round top and it is the most desperate one of the war, but I know very little about it as we are a considerable distance from that point. I am told that there were six thousand that went in to the charge and 1,600 came out. After this charge the battle seems to die away and by 2 o'clock, we retire a short distance and it is evident the Confederates are defeated, though not driven back. We have now had nothing to eat since last night and we are so weak and broken down that we can scarcely stand up because of the intense excitement and danger. But above all is the heart sickening thought of the souls that have been sent to Eternity, many we fear unprepared, and of the many wounded that are still in the throes of agony and death. May God in His infinite mercy comfort them and grant them repentance into life, ere He takes them from earth and comforts the hundreds of people who will have to hear in so short a time that war has done its worst for their loved ones on the front. As for myself, I am a miracle of grace. Here I stand after being so wonderfully protected from the very beginning of the war, my body unharmed and with the Spirit bearing witness with my spirit, that my name is written in the Lamb's Book of Life. With humble gratitude and words, I ask, why, Lord, am I so wonderfully blessed while so many have had to suffer and die this day? My humble prayer is that, for Christ's sake, help me to live henceforth to Thy Service.

The first thing I do now, must be to write home and let my dear parents, sister and brother, know of my safety. For their anxiety and distress concerning my safety after they hear of this tremendous battle, will be misfortunately great, and it may be many days, or even weeks, before my letter can reach them. The mail does not run regularly to Lewisburg now, or any point west of the Allegheny Mountains. Our rations are cooked and brought to us and we bivouac for the night.

The morning of the 4th of July we retire to a fine position and offer the Federals battle, but they fail to advance and seemingly have had enough of us. Our force is tremendous, reported to be 18 or 20 thousand and the Federals' equally as great. A heavy rain sets in lasting 24 hours, but we make ourselves as comfortable as circumstances will permit. For two days and nights our army is still in good spirits and would like to fight. We retire slowly in the direction of Hagerstown and, with Ewell's corps, bring up the rear. The roads are so cut up by the wagon trains that they are almost impassable. The enemy keeps following us, their cavalry keeping at a considerable distance and their infantry out of sight. When we reach Hagerstown we find the Potomac River very high. There we make a stand and I meet some of my acquaintances from Greenbrier belonging to our cavalry. They ask us if we can still fight if the Yankees attack us? We tell them, "of course we will, that is what we are here for." But the Federals soon come to the conclusion, we think, that the better part of valor for them will be to let us alone and we remain here quietly for about two days.

The Potomac gets to a stage that Hill's corps crosses on pontoons at Williamsport, about 5 miles below us, and is brought to our relief, guarding us while we wade the river. It is still high, but with such a large body of men we get along very successfully. At one place I begin to think I will have to swim but get my hand on the shoulder of a very large man, thus steadying me. We made it with our clothes on even though they are thoroughly drenched, but keep our cartridge boxes dry by tying them around our necks and this chokes us nearly to death. This makes the sixth time I wade the Potomac that the water was so deep that it ran in my pocket and stopped my watch. At Hagerstown, William Johnson gives me calico to make me a shirt which is a very acceptable present.

Now we feel as much like fighting than ever because we didn't accomplish what we wished at Gettysburg. We don't acknowledge ourselves defeated although we have lost very heavily indeed. Our appetites have only been whetted by what we have passed through and we long to avenge the deaths of our comrades. Gen. Meade is a prudent commander and I believe he knows better than to bring on another engagement, for I feel from the temper of the men that we will whip them without mercy.

[Editor's note: for reasons unknown, the following brief entries were the only ones written by Edgar for the time period between July, 1863, and January, 1864.]

October, 1863 – I hear of the sudden death of my father from hemorrhage from the lungs. He had been in his usual health when taken with the hemorrhage and died without being able to speak.

September, 1863 - I was made Captain instead of Captain Phil Frazier who was promoted to Major.

November 27, 1863 – Mine Run engagement fought. (I was not in this battle) Confederate victory. After this we go to our winter quarters in Spotsylvania County.

January 1, 1864 - I get my third furlough to go home, but the day is so bitterly cold I stayed in camp until the next day when I start out.

chapter twenty-seven

Captured at Spotsylvania Court House

It is now the 25th of January, 1863, and my furlough has come to an end and I must start back to camp. My brother Tom, takes me on horseback about 60 miles to a point on the valley turnpike to a hotel kept by a man by name of Afrenchains, where I meet the stage that takes me to Bonsacks about 15 miles distant. I arrive safely at the camp I left near Orange Court House and find everything just as I left it. I find many of the boys just getting back from furlough, like myself, and many others just starting home on their furlough, the whole army being furloughed by turns until every man that wished got one. I could have had another in March if I had wished it, but I did not. Going home and leaving again was so that neither I or the family was benefitted by it, so I preferred my soldier life to go on, straight through.

We do not chill much, the ground being wet and muddy and the weather being cold and disagreeable. It was a disadvantage to us to be kept out much, though we are under good military discipline and have our regular religious services Sunday and Wednesday nights. We have some faithful chaplains. The army is still large and officers and men are in good health and spirits. I am now captain of my company but have not more than 25 men present for duty, a few sick, some have deserted, and others on furlough. Confederate money has so depreciated that we feel like it is worth little or nothing. I pay 12 dollars per pound for coffee and 2 dollars for tobacco. For the first time since the war began, I doubt the success of our cause. There is a gloom that hangs over that I cannot expel, try hard as I may. I sense that there is great trouble just ahead for me, and my life as a soldier is going to change. Not that I feel like I'm going to be killed, but some dire calamity. It amounts to a regular premonition. I can no more fight it off than I have power to change the color of my skin. The army is much diminished in numbers, yet the men and officers we have left are just the choice ones, all that are disloyal or inclined to shirk having disappeared by destruction or some other way. So with what men we have left, we could accomplish as much as we ever did.

Time has been dragging on in this same monotonous way and we have now reached the first of May at which time Grant's army is on the move and is crossing the Rappahannock, and of course, we will soon be astir again. We now have cooked two or three days' rations and are ready to march at a moment's warning and we hear the firing of our cavalry. The whole army is ordered forward by the 4th. Grant's powerful army is over the river and on the 5th he makes an attack on Longstreet. A bloody battle ensues in which neither side gains any advantage that I can see, but great loss of life. On the 6th he moves against our side and makes an attack on our corps, with great fury, which is repulsed, we losing some good and gallant officers, amongst them Major Frazier. Grant with his bulldog courage keeps moving to our right and at the same time strengthening his lines. As fast as his men and officers are killed and wounded he brings up fresh recruits. It is now the 10th and he attacks us again. This attack is more successful than the two former attacks.

Now for the first time since the war we are in breastworks and it brings to my mind vividly what Stonewall Jackson always said about men fighting from behind breastworks, and we feel the truth of what he said just now. We are now attacked on the left with powerful force, but not in our front and not enfilading fire.

Dale's Brigade, which is on our left, gives way and the enemy comes over the breastworks and goes two or three hundred yards directly in our rear. They are only checked by our reinforcements and then are back over our breastworks again. We find that we have made a very great mess of the enemy, some of the men counted 6,000 dead bodies in front of Dale's Brigade. We are still holding our line, but believe we could have made more of a success if we had not been behind breastworks. This ends the fighting on the 10th and we are beginning to find Grant, a good match for us, way ahead of the Federal army that we have had to contend with before. Up to this time we have had no trouble in driving them back over the river, but now they are much more stubborn. This fact is noticed and remarked on by many of our men.

It is now night, and our rations are cooked and brought to us by men detailed for the purpose and we sleep on our arms. It is snowing on the 11th and we do no fighting. But we know from the noise and different movement, that Grant is preparing for a greater and more vigorous attack than ever. Before night he has lines so near us that we have to draw in our skirmishers. It is nearly night and we rest on our arms, feeling that the morning must surely bring bloodshed and carnage. I feel an unaccountable and gloomy premonition that great trouble is just before me and can sleep none at all after 12 o'clock and sit up on the breastworks. Just at the first dawn of day, Grant's thirty thousand marched against us, formed in nine columns deep and more toward our breastworks, with a yell they hurl their greatest fury against the brigades on our right capturing the works and bayoneting many of our men. After this takes place we have serious apprehensions of our safety and soon we see the "bluecoats" coming down on our right and know that they have captured our men. Everything is now in the wildest confusion. Our field officers are all either killed, wounded or missing. They have disappeared at any rate, and we have no orders at all. The enemy is nearly at our backs but still we cling to the hope that two brigades are supporting us, but alas they never come, although they were placed there to strengthen our weak points. Our flag is now shot off the staff, but the color bearer has presence of mind enough to hide it in the breastwork by sticking it out of sight. By this time we see that the enemy is actually surrounding us in front and back, demanding our surrender, and we feel that further resistance is useless. They order us to throw down our arms but in the confusion I fail to throw down my sword. The first thing I am aware of is a burly Dutchman swinging at me with his bayonet and, of course, I made no delay in dropping my sword. Just at this time I notice my old friend and neighbor, Walter Preston, coming towards me with his left arm shot almost entirely off, just hanging by the skin. I have time only to barely speak to him when he is called away by a Federal surgeon and we are all marched rapidly to the enemy's rear and I see no more of him.

When we get there we are amazed to see what multitudes of the enemy are there and how very near they have been to us the night before. Among these troops there are many negroes, who tell us if they had their way they would soon put an end to us. We pass near Gen. Grant's headquarters, and we are shocked as we see what vast numbers of us have been captured, more than one half of the Stonewall Brigade. I cannot now refrain from speaking of what I think is another great mistake of Gen. Lee's in leaving his troops in such an exposed position, it being an angle of the breastworks and is from this time called "the bloody angle." We now march straight through until we get to Fredericksburg, and on the way we meet at least 10,000 fresh troops, coming to reinforce their army, all well clothed, and in a fine condition just fairly shining. I remarked often to our men that day, that "there is no possible chance for us to go on with all that wealth and such numbers to back the enemy."

We go to camp at Fredericksburg and there meet thousands more prisoners of war, who have been captured only a few days before. In the morning the rain is coming down and we are loaded on steamboats and start for Ft. Delaware. Our voyage is as pleasant as could be expected under the circumstances. Our guard consists of old veterans who have been wounded and treat us with as much consideration as we could expect. It takes us two days to make the voyage. The boats are comfortable enough but we are very much crowded. When we arrive at Ft. Delaware, our persons are examined and all our effects taken from us but our clothing. I had silver which was taken from me and I also had two dollars in Confederate money which I exchanged for 10 cents in greenbacks. I also had a small piece of tobacco that I am allowed to keep. We are marched at once to the barracks where we meet with quite a number of Confederate prisoners who are very glad to see and ask us many questions about the affairs in the Confederacy. Many of them have been here even since the battle of Gettysburg and are extremely attentive to us and give us anything they have that will add to our comfort, which cheers us up wonderfully. We had one man who was captured at the same time I was who had 15 dollars in gold, and when his person was searched, he put it in his mouth and thus kept it. His name is Lieutenant Preston from southwest Alabama.

As soon as we get here the officers are separated from the privates, put in different barracks, and never get to see anything more of each other. It does not take us long to accustom ourselves to prison life. I am surprised how easily we do it. The prison ration is very inadequate to our wants. We are marched to the table once a day and get a piece of baker's bread, a pint of soup, and a small piece of half spoiled beef. After being here for a while we refuse all the rations except the bread, and men pretend to eat at the table but take our bread to our bunks when many of us who had a little money, could buy anything we wanted to eat from a sutler. This we added to our bread and made a comfortable fare. A great many of us had friends and relations living inside of the Confederate lines and soon got money to answer our purpose as well as clothing and tobacco. There was a great deal of clothing and tobacco sent to us from the ladies of Baltimore. Most of us try to content ourselves and make the best of prison life, yet a few seem to be very miserable and do not try to get any comfort out of anything.

Time drags on without anything worth mentioning. It is now the first of June and we hear the familiar shout "fresh fish" and we see that some more prisoners are being brought in. We are always anxious to see them and get information about our army and by this information hear that our flag that we hid in the breastworks was found and taken care of. I am exceedingly anxious to hear from my dear home. I have never heard a word from there since I was captured although I write every four or five days. We are much crowded and the weather exceedingly hot. We sleep on beds with nothing to make it comfortable, but a blanket. We have a good deal of reading matter and occasionally get a northern paper.

It is about the first of June and a great religious interest commences in the prison. We have some distinguished preachers with us, such as Dr. Handy from Norfolk, Virginia. He is being held as a hostage. He is Presbyterian and we have a very fine Methodist preacher, a Baptist preacher, and others of smaller note. We have services every day and all denominations join in with us but the Episcopalians. It certainly did look strange to me, them holding a little service off to themselves once a week, on every Sunday. All the others of us are so enthused over the way the Holy Spirit is being poured out on us and worship daily.

chapter twenty-eight

PRISON LIFE

This prison life is not only endurable, but even bright sometimes. There are those coming to Christ every day and at the end of three or four weeks from 50 to 75 have come and bowed and acknowledged themselves on the Lord's side. My humble self is among that number, but it is what I have been willing to do ever since my experience on that terrible battlefield of Gettysburg. The way we make this profession is that Dr. Handy asks all of us that felt our sins have been bathed away by the blood of Jesus Christ to come forward. He with the other ministers questioned us as to our spiritual experience, and our preference of churches and a list of our names were taken. The most often mentioned preference is Methodist. I, of course, being raised a staunch Presbyterian am of that list. After this we have religious services regularly twice every week, which are exceedingly interesting and instructive. Dr. Handy, I think, is one of the very finest preachers I have ever listened to.

It is now about the 1st day of July and I receive money from my relatives in Kentucky, Dr. Whitaker and his wife, who was a Miss Withrow, from Lewisburg. Money is being sent to my fellow prisoners, and there are thousands of dollars here, which makes our living very comfortable at present.

It is about the 20th and an order comes for 50 field officers to be taken south for what purpose we don't know just now, but in a very short time we hear that they have been exchanged, which elates us very much. Time plays on in the same monotonous way until the 20th of August and another order came for 600 officers to come into line and we are actually rejoiced thinking our fate will be the same as that of the field officers. We are called out in line. Our names are read out in alphabetical order and we are ordered to return to the barracks and be ready to report when called for, which is an hour or two.

All is now bustle and confusion and everyone thinking it a most fortunate change for us and we are pitying the ones we leave behind us and give them all our valuable clothing that we are not actually using.

The time comes for us to start and we are marched out, crowded on a boat like so many cattle or sheep. The weather is mighty hot and we suffer dreadfully from the heat and being so crowded. We are guarded by a man of war and about 100 Federal officers on the boat with us to keep us from getting unruly. We are pressing near the southern coast most of the way, though at one time while on the North Carolina coast, we were 50 miles from shore for a whole day. I am today very sea sick and can truthfully say it is the worst sickness I have ever experienced on the Hatteras and Lookout, North Carolina coast. After five days we run into Charleston Harbor where the vessel is anchored and we are kept for ten days. Our crowded condition and the hot climate make the heat almost beyond endurance and the wonder is we are not all sick. We get no fresh air and the water we get to drink is nothing but sea water, with the salt taken out and what is worst of all, we have just found out that we are doomed to be disappointed in our hope to be exchanged. Instead we are taken off and placed on Morris Island, inside of a high stockade. We are to be retaliated on by being exposed to the fire from the Confederate batteries for an offense of having taken six hundred of their officers from Andersonville and putting them under the fire of their own guns in the city of Charleston. This was done purely in self defense as they were placed in a part of the city where there were only women and children and the Federals were firing on that very portion of the city. They were only left there two days, and worst of all, we are guarded by a negro regiment and the colonel, though a white man, is the meanest looking man I ever saw and treats us worse than his Negro subordinates.

We are now half way between two Yankees batteries. Our men, of course, knowing we are here, fire with the most perfect accuracy I ever saw, pouring their mortar shells right in to the Federals battery, doing us little damage. Though occasionally, a stray piece of shell lights among us. One piece of shell went through the tent I was occupying. Three of our men are slightly wounded with these pieces of shells. While we stay here, three others are shot by Negro sentinels, for the slightest offenses. The firing from neither our batteries or that of the Federals is constant, but every evening about sundown until nine or ten, both open with terrific fury and notwithstanding our helpless and dangerous situation, we actually view with admiration and enthusiasm the magnificent brilliance shown by those mortar shells as they circle around high up in the air and burst near the ground. The show is grand in the extreme.

Our rations are nothing but hard-tack and bacon, but our sleeping accommodations are better than at Ft. Delaware. We have tents and sleep on the soft dry sand. We are not allowed to have any assistance from friends outside, as we were at Ft. Delaware, except the ladies of Charleston are allowed to send us six hundred pounds of tobacco, which most of us stood much in need of. The great two-hundred pound balls from the enemy's guns pass over us, on their way to a poor old target, about 20 or 30 feet above our heads, but do us no harm.

Time passes on in this same routine for six weeks and until, I suppose, they are satisfied with this kind of retaliation. We are sent to Ft. Pulaski, Georgia, and it is about the 10th of October when we are to be retaliated on by starving us. We are crowded in the old dirty fort, which is damp and disagreeable, and we stay a month or five weeks. Our rations here are crackers, but I got about as much as my appetite called for of just that one thing. Any mail that we get is six weeks coming and much of it never reaches us at all. One day as we are called out in line to receive our mail, my name is called and a letter is held up. My heart sinks when I see it is marked in mourning. When I open it, I find the sad announcement of my dear mother's death, which does not surprise me much, as I left her in such a weak state of health and so distressed over my dear father's death. What a stricken family mine now is. Father and mother now dead and me in prison. I am afraid my sister Delia will scarcely live through it all.

Now November comes in, and the weather is very cold and damp. Just at this time the Yankees take our U.S. blankets from us and I was so unfortunate to have one of that kind, although all those that had Confederate blankets were allowed to keep them. The place we are in is as damp as a cellar and we have to sleep on the bricks of the fort. I have nothing in the shape of a wrap but an oil cloth, which gave me a very deep cold. There are very many others just as badly off as I am, though my cold takes a very dangerous form, settling on my bowels giving me chronic diarrhea. As we are so crowded here, the Yankees concluded to take part of us to Hilton Head, South Carolina. It is sometimes called Port or Fort Royal. We are not so much crowded and in dry quarters, but I'm getting gradually weaker and have no medical aid because I've never reported on the sick list. I have such a horror of a hospital, but over 100 have so reported and been taken there. Maybe it would be better for me if I could make up my mind to do it also.

Our rations are now cut down to ten ounces of sour corn meal a day, and pickles. A frightful diet for a person in my condition. We are allowed no utensils for cooking and not even a chip in the way of fuel, but we manage to find little bits of wood on the beach under the sand that we dug up from under the sand with our hands. We broke our canteens to pieces and took one side of them to boil our sour meal into mush. This keeps life going, but after a while the mush turns entirely against me in my weak condition and for four days at one time I didn't take a bite of food. So in this extremity I told the man that cooks for the sick prisoners of my condition and he advised me by all means to go to the hospital. Still I refused, so he seems to have sympathy for me and allows me to come into the room he has his cook stove in and gives me the refused pieces of bread the men leave on the plate and a cup of coffee occasionally, and allows me to get warm at his stove. This helps me some though it continues only a short time. We are not allowed a bit of meat and are driven to such extremities that some with weak stomachs may have their sensibilities shocked when I say, which is a fact, that we actually did eat cats and rats. I know of one fat dog that was killed and cooked, but I did not eat any of him. I did eat a piece of a cat and also of a rat and it really was not so bad, but was helpful to our poor weak and impoverished stomachs, as we had tasted nothing like meat for forty days. The taste of the cat was not unlike that of a squirrel and the rat was still more palatable and had the flavor of a squirrel, than the cat had.

I must speak of another part of our suffering and that will probably be disgusting to some, and that is the army lice that I have referred to before in the early part of the war. We now have more of them than ever and they distress us much more for we have no way to boil our clothes. Although we can wash them in cold water, that does not destroy the lice. Nothing but boiling will do that, so the lice are actually enough to kill us without starvation. When we put on clean clothes, or what we call clean, it does not make the matter any better, for the lice are still there.

I am still without a blanket and I suffer for the want of it more than I can tell. So I cut the gutta-percha buttons off my coat, take the little piece that is inlaid on knife handles, cut it in pieces of any shape I want, and make sets for finger rings, making the rings out of the buttons I cut off my coat. I cut them out until they are large enough to go on a man's finger. I succeed very well in making four rings, putting the sets in them. Of the little pieces of metal, some I cut in heart shape and some in other shapes. I inlay the sets and polish the rings that I have made. I sell the four rings for five dollars, enough to buy me a nice double U.S. blanket, and I feel like I am rich. It is surprising at the ready sale we find for these rings. We sell them to the Yankees and they send them home to their families as curiosities and mementos of the work of the rebel prisoners. The only way we make these rings out of buttons, was by keeping our pocket knives very sharp. In that way we could make a surprisingly nice polished ring after rubbing them thoroughly with sand paper.

We are fairly into the winter now, it being some time in December. The weather is very disagreeable and damp, although there is no snow. Time drags on slowly and without any comfort to us, especially in the way of rations. I, of course, find my blanket a great comfort to me. I am some encouraged about my health although I am getting weak. It is as much as I can do to get up to my bunk, which is only about eight feet from the floor. And now, about the middle of January, we have considerable excitement in the prison by three men trying to make their escape. They deluded the first sentinel in some way, got by him and made their way to the beach, deceiving all the sentinels. They had captured a little boat when they were discovered and brought back, put in close confinement and they, as well as ourselves, are watched more closely than ever.

There are a great many sick and in the hospital. We just feel like our very lives are worn out and so time drags on and it seems sometimes like we cannot stand the hardships much longer. In February, we hear that the Federal government is going to confer with the Confederate government about a cessation of hostilities. The Commission is to meet at Hampton Roads and we are much interested, for we hope there will be some hope of peace made. Ever since my capture, very often I see how well equipped the Federal army is, much better than ours.

The 12th of March comes and four hundred of us are able to travel. Fifty of us are loaded on a boat and we are told we are being taken back to Ft. Delaware, which very much encourages us and we feel like maybe we can see Dixie again. One man dies on the boat and his body is thrown overboard. We have a very rough and dangerous voyage, the waves running high and wild most of the time. The vessel is not overly safe, it not being a sea going one, but only suitable to use on the coast. While we are on the coast of North Carolina, the seas are especially rough and dangerous. We arrive at Ft. Delaware in safety and we sick men stand the trip well. Any of us that will are permitted to go to the hospital.

We find now a most wonderful change for the better and it seems like we have reached a paradise compared to what we have left. We are taken one by one to a nice bathroom and thoroughly bathed by a nurse and the clothes we had were taken from us and replaced by nice clean under clothing only. The building we are in is about 100 feet long with four stoves in it. Fifty of us sick men are put in this building and each one of us are furnished with a nice comfortable cot, consisting of a straw mattress, sheet, pillow, and covering sufficient to keep us warm. The cots are placed three feet apart. A great number are very ill, much worse off than I am. The men are afflicted with different diseases. There is some scurvy and diarrhea. We who have the latter get a toddy every morning before breakfast, and for breakfast a piece of toast, a soft boiled egg, and a cup of coffee. Two ounces of whiskey were allowed for each toddy, but I had to get the nurse to give me just half that quantity as the full allowance made me so drunk, I could not raise my head up. Those who have scurvy get a vegetable diet. In a short time the man on each side of me dies, one in a week and the other in two weeks. Anyone may know it makes me feel a little discouraged, though I do not know what the diseases were they died of. We have four nurses in this ward, and the physician comes around every morning. One poor fellow, Lieutenant Franks, I am especially interested in. His mother, who lives in Winchester, came through the lines and is allowed to stay with him. He is very sick with diarrhea and in a week or two he dies. He has been near me all the time and I have seen a great deal of him.

I continue to improve and everything has gone on smoothly until now comes the 4th of April, and we are shocked at the startling announcement made to us in a formal, official manner, that Richmond has fallen. One hundred guns are fired from the fort by the Federal government in exultation over their success and the downfall of the Confederacy. I am not as much surprised as some of the other prisoners, for actually, ever since my capture I have had my doubts of the success of the Confederacy. Now the next thing comes on the 10th of May, 1864, which is the surrender at Appomattox Courthouse. It is exulted over by the Yankees more than the fall of Richmond. A hundred guns are again fired from the fort in honor and exultation of the event. Everything moves on here in the hospital about as usual for a week longer and we hear of the assassination of President Lincoln, which causes the Yankees to treat us pretty gruffly. We fear it may still cause worse treatment towards us, but we never notice very much change.

Now comes about the 20th of April and the weather is getting very pleasant and warm. As I look out on the shores, it makes me feel home sick, although I reckon we have more reason to hope for getting home sooner than ever. Nature seems healthful and refreshing to our eyes, a so long enduring prison life. Between the 1st and 10th of May, I am able to get out to the barracks, where I meet many of my old friends and acquaintances. I very much enjoy it but the fare and lodging is not, of course, near as good as I have had in the hospital. Among some of the young men I meet is Dick George, a cousin of mine from southwest Virginia. I am told that Col. Edgar, Major Woodrum, and Wash McDowell were captured at Cold Harbor, but got exchanged because they were sick.

We are now getting very restless and anxious, the surrender having taken place a month or more ago and no hope of our release. We do not understand the reason, and to add to our anxiety, we hear various kinds of reports concerning what is going to be done with prisoners, officers especially. It is now the 10th of June and we are rejoiced. An order comes for all the prisoners who were captured in 1863 to be released, and for all such to get ready to start. They do so with alacrity and leave with the most enthusiastic cheers, the rest of us left behind wishing them a happy return to Dixie. On the 15th an order comes that prisoners captured in 1864, up to the 1st of May, to be released, which is done. And on the 17th our time comes and about 10:00 a.m. we bid our adieu to Ft. Delaware forever, which is Saturday morning. We go by steamer to Havre De Grace, Maryland. There we wait about an hour for a train to take us to Baltimore. The Federals give us transportation and rations to our nearest railroad station. It seems unnatural for us not to have the Yankee bayonets at our back. We actually have to get used to being free. We have a nice pleasant run to Baltimore, which place we reach about dark, where we remain until next evening, Sunday. We then take a boat for Richmond and reach there sometime during the day Tuesday, and owing to irregularity of trains, we do not get away until Thursday, so I have opportunity to look about the city. It presents a melancholy aspect compared to what it did when I was here in 1862. I walk over a part of the burnt district which makes a doleful appearance and I begin to realize that Dixie is in a ruined and devastating condition.

chapter twenty-nine

RETURNING HOME

On Thursday we come as far as Staunton, where we spend the night at American Hotel, as we all have a little money. Our little squad now begins to feel like we can separate. Up to this time, we have all felt a strange fascination to stick together, having been in the enemy's country so long but now we feel like we are among friends again and can scatter out. We are disappointed to find there will be no train to Jackson's River depot for 6 days, so we all start out on foot. Two of the officers of the Allegheny Rifles and officers from the Greenbrier Sharpshooters begin walking. After we have walked 20 miles and about the middle of the afternoon, Captain Morris of Edgar's Battalion and his sister-in-law Miss Dolan, who had been to Albemarle County on a visit, overtook us. When they found out who I am, they offer me a seat in their carriage, which I gladly accepted, as I have not yet recovered my strength after my severe illness in prison.

After three days travel, we arrive at Dry Creek. There I spend the night with a friend, Mr. Kerr, and walked from there to Lewisburg and got my dinner at Cousin John Withrow's,

Returning Home

where I am received with open arms and all the kindness and affection lavished on me that possibly could be. By the time I am through with dinner, Cousin James Withrow, who also lives in Lewisburg, has heard of my arrival and sends a horse over for me to ride home. I had expected to walk but this thoughtfulness of Cousin James is most timely, for I am by no means strong and I thankfully accept the kindness and am soon on the old familiar home road. But alas, how the joy of getting home is saddened by the thought that my dear father and mother are both gone from earth. I do not sorrow as "thou who has no hope," for I can look forward to meeting them again in our heavenly home, where there will be no more parting. I am now in sight of my home, but notice no one out on the premises. I strain my eyes to catch a glimpse of any person or animal that may be moving about. The natural scenery about the old homestead is just as beautiful as I have always remembered seeing it. Never has it seemed more attractive and homelike to me than it does now. The rich green summer foliage that drapes the large trees in the yard and thickly wooded hills brings back vividly to my mind my happy boyhood. The fences are out of repair and there is a scarcity of stock as I look over the fields, showing the ravages of war. Yet it is now past, and I am almost home again. I feel like my cup of happiness is full and that it could not be made to hold another drop of bliss. My heart actually seems to be breaking with utter joy and, for the moment, I lose sight of the sad truth that my dear parents are both gone. I have now turned the last corner in the lane that leads up to the front gate and I see Ann, one of our faithful colored girls who has never left us, at the well drawing water. As I come near the big gate that opens in the lane that leads to the stables, she looks up, and recognizing me, sounds the clarion note that "Master Alfred is coming." Then I see more signs of life around the house by the time I get to the gate and off my horse. My poor little sister Delia is nearly half way up the walk meeting me. I say little sister, although she is 17 years old, yet she is the youngest of the family and has always been the pet with all of us, but most especially was she of my father's and mine. Now she has grieved so deeply over the loss of our dear parents and felt such anxiety about me during my prison life, that she looks to me almost like a shadow.

My own heart aches for her as I catch her in my arms just in time to prevent her from falling to the ground, which I would not be able to do if she was much more than a mite of humanity. My own strength is just about gone by this time, partly because of my weak physical condition, but to a great extent arising from my extreme joy at reaching home, and then for the first time realizing fully how thoroughly our home is broken by the loss of our dear parents. Now we are at the porch and are met by my two older sisters, Lizzie (Mrs. Creigh) and Carrie. Much to my encouragement they look to be in good health and are cheerful. We sit down in the sitting room and rejoice over my return and I feel like it is home after all the sad surrounding. I begin to feel some of that same enthusiastic joy that I felt on my way from Lewisburg here. Now my brother Tom has heard I have come and is here to welcome me, but alas, he feels so deeply the death of our dear parents, he is almost as melancholy as Delia. I am beginning to realize sure enough that my dear parents are gone from earth, something I could not do while in the army and in prison. I would read and re-read the letter I received from home telling me of their deaths but could not realize it. It distressed me more than I can tell for it seemed like it must be indifference.

Appendix A

LETTER FROM ILLINOIS RELATIVE WHILE PRISONER OF WAR

Rushville, Ill., June 9th, 1864

My dear Alfred

Your letter to your Cousin Marion came duly to hand by last mail, and we were all very glad to hear of and from you, notwithstanding we regret your present unfortunate position, and hope it may be made as comfortable to you as circumstances will permit as we doubt not it will be. We send you by express tomorrow morning addressed as you direct a small box containing a few articles of clothing which we trust may be acceptable and useful to wit, one coat, 2 pairs of pants, 2 shirts, 2 pairs of drawers, two pairs of socks, and two or three collars and some other articles. We hope they will reach you in season. We would be very glad on account of our high regard for your parents as well as for yourself to render you any assistance we could to make your present condition as comfortable as possible that we could do consistent with our obligation to the government and the regulations that surround you. We will be glad to hear from you on receipt of the box and if there are any articles that you specially need do not fail to let us know. Would a small amount of money be useful and would it be admissible?

Our oldest son is a Lieutenant in Co. I, 119th Regiment of Ill. Vol. (Edwin M. Anderson). We have just heard that he was wounded in a battle on the Red River about 16 miles from its mouth (the wound was slight). Your letter gave us the first intimation that we had near and dear friends on both sides of the bloody contest and it may be that the soldier of today may be the prisoner of tomorrow.

Hoping that this war may be brought to a speedy close and that friends may be again united, all enmities reconciled. All the family desire to be affectionately remembered to you. We were very sorry to hear of the death of your dear father. Your letter was the first intimation from friends in Virginia for more than three years.

Vy Affectionately Yours
James L. Anderson

Appendix B

Post-War Love Letter to Lydia McNeel

At home Monday evening 17th August

My dearest little Darling,

I reckon you will think I am rather slow when I tell you that it was an hour after dark when I got home, and oh you don't know how badly I had the "blues" all the way down. All the energy that I could possibly command was scarcely sufficient to keep me up. It was certainly the longest evening I ever experienced. I am sure you can't help being real sorry for me for you know you are the only cause of all the sufferings of my poor heart. I know it is wrong in me to become so desponding after leaving you but I can't help it. Don't think that I am doubting the sincerity of your dear little heart by my getting so desponding for that is one of the most prominent characteristics of my nature. I could not doubt you, don't think that such a thing ever entered my head. How full of hope I look forward to the time when we can be always together and it will not be necessary for me to go through all the trouble of being separated from you.

I often wonder if there was ever a man who gave his heart more completely to a Lady than mine has been given to you. I don't believe there ever was. Could it be doubted?

I met Wash. Livesay on my way down (he and I both travel the old road you know) and his looks betrayed him at once. He reminded me a good deal of myself. Since then I have determined that I would not look so "sheepish" when anyone met me. I certainly know how to sympathize with the poor creature. We poor men have a hard time of it doing our courting and then when our little Demoiselles happen to say "no" (as some in yours and my knowledge have done) it drives us almost to desperation or perhaps to Texas. I do think men are so foolish when they are courting. You Ladies ought always be sorry for them and help them along a little by when you know they have fixed themselves to "pop" the question. Don't you wish you would have know when I was going to court you? I don't believe you could have talked me out of it, as you did Bob Moffett that Sunday. Wish I could see him. I would throw a little light on the subject when Ladies become unmanageable.

I hope you think of me often. It seems like an age before the first of September but you must write to me promptly and keep me cheered up and I will try to not give way to my gloomy disposition. I feel that you are the only one that can give me real happiness in this world.

Ever your devoted lover
Alfred Edgar

Present my compliments to Miss Lucy if she knows you get this letter. Please accept a kiss which I mean to be just as full of love as though I gave it to you in person.

In June, 1875, Captain Edgar married Lydia McNeel, daughter of Col. Paul McNeel of Hillsboro, West Virginia. (Photo courtesy of Allan N. Clower, Ronceverte, West Virginia)

Appendix C

Obituary of Captain Alfred Mallory Edgar

by Rev. James C. Johnson

Alfred M. Edgar was born July 10th, 1837, in the ancestral home of the family at Edgar's Mill, now the site of Ronceverte, Greenbrier County, West Virginia. His parents were Archer Mathews Edgar and his wife Nancy Howe Pearis. From this mother of French Hugenot extraction he inherited a gentle manner and indomnitable courage. He attended the school in Lewisburg founded and conducted by Dr. McElhenny which was influential in forming the character and directing the lives of so many men. About the time Mr. Edgar reached maturity his country was rent with civil war, and he was among the first of his community to volunteer, enlisting in Company E, 27th Virginia Regiment, which was afterward attached to what became the famous "Stonewall Brigade." Mr. Edgar enthusiastically followed the fortunes of the Brigade under their incomparable leader, "Stonewall" Jackson, in the forced marches, the rapid flanking movements, and bold charges characteristic of his generalship. He was wounded at Port Republic on the 8th of June, 1862, and in addition to this wound, carried to his grave evidences of the rapid marching made by Jackson's "Foot Cavalry."

Mr. Edgar was several times promoted and in September, 1863, he became captain of his company. He was in all the important engagements in which his command took part until the battles of the Wilderness. During those trying days he was in the forefront of Lee's hard-pressed forces until the severe engagement that raged at the "Bloody Angle." The Stonewall

Appendix C

Brigade, veterans of Fredericksburg, Chancellorsville, and Antietam, were defendants of "the Salient" and against them Grant hurled division after division. Finally, Burnside's Corps, in overwhelming numbers, swept across the defense of the Confederates within the "Bloody Angle" and captured four thousand prisoners. Among this number was Captain Edgar. This was on May 12, 1864. He was taken to Fort Delaware and held there as a prisoner until under the retaliatory measures of the North, he, in a body of six hundred Confederate officers, was taken to Morris Island, near Charleston, South Carolina, and exposed to the fire of Confederate guns. On the 17th of June, 1865, he was released from prison, and sick and well nigh helpless from the hardships of prison life, he made his way home, reaching there the 26th of June, too feeble to leave unaided the stage coach. During his absence his father and mother had died and the feeble and discouraged soldier came home to find a lonely hearthstone and new economic conditions. Like thousands of returned veterans he addressed himself resolutely to the task of conserving the shattered fortunes of the family and adjusting himself to the changed condition that the war had brought.

He lived quietly in Greenbrier County until June, 1875, when he married Miss Lydia, daughter of Col. Paul McNeel, and thereafter took up his residence in the Little Levels of Pocahontas County., there to spend the remaining years of life in the quiet pursuits of farmer and stock raiser.

Captain Edgar received religious impressions during his life in the army, but did not make a profession of his faith until 1866, when he united with the Old Stone Church, Lewisburg, West Virginia. As a Christian, he was modest and unassuming as in everything else. He shrank from personal activity in the church, but bore his testimony by a faithful attendance on public worship and scrupulous honesty in all his dealings. During the 38 years of his residence in the Little Levels he had not missed a single Communion Service until his last illness necessitated his absence. He was conscientious and frank in all his relations with his fellow man, and always ready to cover their faults with a charitable forbearance. His leading traits of character were humility and love of peace. He thus came within the scope of two beatitudes, "Blessed are the meek," and "Blessed are the peace-makers."

His last illness was long but not painful and was borne with cheerful patience. He entered peacefully into rest on the morning of October 8, 1913. After simple memorial services in the home, October 10th, conducted by his pastor, Rev. J.C. Johnson, assisted by Revs. A.S. Rachal of Marlinton, and W.F. Lowance, accompanied by an escort of Confederate veterans and a large gathering of friends and relatives, he was laid to rest in McNeel Cemetery.

There remain to feel most keenly his loss his widow and five children – three daughters, Mrs. F.R. Hill, of Marlinton, Mrs. H.W. McNeel, of Academy, and Miss Rachel, at home, – and two sons, Mr. Allan P., Esquire, of Marlinton, and Mr. George, at home. "Thou shalt go to thy grave in a full age as a shock of corn cometh in its season."

[Source: Clower family papers, Ronceverte, West Virginia]

APPENDIX C

Grave Marker of Captain Alfred Mallory Edgar, in McNeel Family Cemetery, Pocahontas County, West Virginia. Note that his middle name has only one L on the marker, even though family documents include the original marker request which indicated the spelling as Mallory.

[Photo courtesy of Allan N. Clower, Ronceverte, West Virginia]

Appendix D

Alfred Mallory Edgar

Service Record in the 27th Virginia Infantry, CSA

Captain, Co. E. Born at Edgar's Mill (now Ronceverte), Greenbrier County, 7/10/1837. Enlisted at Lewisburg, 5/9/1861, as Private. Present until elected 4th Corporal, 6/27/1861. Present until absent on leave, 2/16/1862, for 25 days. Present until elected 2nd Lt., 4/23/1862. Present until elected Captain, 9/28/1863. Present until wounded in action (left shoulder) and captured, Spotsylvania Court House, 5/12/1864. Sent to Fort Delaware. One of the "Immortal 600." Released 6/16/1865. Height: 5 ft., 9 inches; dark complexion, dark hair, blue eyes. Farmer and Stockman, Greenbrier County. Died in Pocahontas County, West Virginia, 10/8/1913.

Source: Compiled Service Records of Confederate Soldiers Who Served in Organizations from the State of Virginia, The National Archives.

Appendix E

SERVICE OF THE 27TH VIRGINIA INFANTRY, CSA

The 27th Infantry Regiment was organized in May, 1861, and accepted into Confederate service in July. The men were from the counties of Alleghany, Rockbridge, Monroe, Greenbrier, and Ohio. It contained only eight companies and became part of the famous Stonewall Brigade. During the war it served under the command of General T.J. Jackson, R.B. Garnett, Winder, Paxton, J.A. Walker, and W. Terry. The 27th fought at First Manassas, First Kernstown, and in Jackson's Valley Campaign. It then participated in the campaign of the Army of Northern Virginia from the Seven Days' Battles to Cold Harbor, moved with Early to the Shenandoah Valley, and was active around Appomattox. The regiment reported 141 casualties at First Manassas, 57 at First Kernstown, and 4 of the 136 engaged at First Winchester. It lost 3 killed at Cedar Mountain, had 4 killed and 23 wounded at Second Manassas, and sustained 9 killed and 62 wounded at Chancellorsville. Of the 148 in action at Gettysburg about thirty percent were disabled. Only 1 officer and 20 men surrendered. The field officers were Colonels John Echols, James K. Edmondson, William A. Gordon, and A.J. Grisby; Lieutenant Colonels Charles L. Haynes and Daniel M. Shriver; and Majors Philip F. Frazer and Elisha F. Paxton.

Source: National Park Service Civil War Soldiers and Sailors System

Appendix F

Further Reading:
27th Virginia Infantry, by Lowell Reidenbaugh
Stonewall Brigade, by James I. Robertson, Jr.

Appendix F

THE EDGAR HOUSE TODAY: THE EDGARTON INN BED AND BREAKFAST

"*Edgarton*"

Edgarton, a fine example of Queen Anne style architecture, incorporates an earlier circa 1810 dwelling built by Thomas Edgar, grandfather of Captain Alfred Mallory Edgar, and founder of the Ronceverte settlement then known as St. Lawrence Ford. Colonel Cecil C. Clay, who formed the Ronceverte Development Corporation for the incorporation of the town of Ronceverte in 1882, lived in this house. Colonel Ellery C. Best, superintendent of the St. Lawrence Boom and Lumber Company, lived here and added the Victorian architecture to the building circa 1885.

Appendix F

Today, Edgarton is a bed and breakfast operated by proprietor Kathy King. For more information on visiting the Edgarton Inn, visit www.edgartoninn.com.